PERSONALITIES AROUND DAVID

# PERSONALITIES AROUND DAVID

## HOLMES ROLSTON

**JOHN KNOX PRESS**
Richmond, Virginia

Unless otherwise indicated, Scripture quotations
are from the *Revised Standard Version of the Bible,*
copyrighted 1946 and 1952.

# DEDICATION

Dedicated to the congregation of the Hawkins Memorial Presbyterian Church of Ford, Virginia. It was during the time that I served as supply pastor of this church that most of these character studies of the personalities around David were prepared.

# FOREWORD

David and the men and women who gather around him constitute one of the most arresting galaxies of characters to be found in the pages of Holy Scripture or, indeed, in all literature. There is a depth of human interest here that has seldom been surpassed, and as we begin to study these characters and live with them we see actual persons of three thousand years ago in the encounter with the God who made himself known to Israel.

In these studies I have sought to portray the personalities around David in the context of their world and in their abiding significance for all mankind.

Holmes Rolston

# CONTENTS

# 1

## THE AGE OF DAVID—three thousand years ago and relevant to life today

"The God in whose hand is your breath, and whose are all your ways . . ." (Daniel 5:23).

If some observer from Tyre had contemplated the fate of Israel after the victory of the Philistines at Mount Gilboa, he would have been certain that the cause of Israel was lost. It would have seemed to him that the future of Palestine was with the Philistines. Over a period of many years there had been a struggle between the children of Israel and the Philistines for a dominant position in Palestine. At times it had looked as if the Israelites under Samuel or Saul might win. But after the defeat of Israel on Mount Gilboa and with it the death of Saul and his son Jonathan, the power of Israel appeared to be broken. The Philistines overran almost the whole of western Palestine. The best that Abner, captain of the armies of Saul, could do was to set up a token kingdom on the far side of Jordan. Israel and Judah were divided, and David's rule in Judah was exercised with the permission of the Philistines.

Ten years later the whole picture had changed. The children of Israel had found in David a leader who was able to bring unity to the twelve tribes. In two decisive battles, the Philistines had been crushed. The nations around about Israel had reacted in fear to the spectacle of a strong and united Israel. But one by one they had gone down in defeat before Israel. The beginning of the struggle with the nations around about Israel was with the Ammonites. When the Ammonites found that they were losing the war, they called for aid from the Syrians to the north. But both the Ammonites and the Syrians were conquered. A garrison of Israel was in Damascus. These victories were followed by victories over Moab and Edom. For the first and last time in her history, Israel was in full possession of the promised land. There followed a period of history known as the golden age in the life of Israel. It was a long period of peace and prosperity in which the creative energies of a people came to full expression. The Ark of the Lord was brought to Jerusalem, and this city was made a center of worship for all Israel. Later, in the time of Solomon, the temple of the Lord was built there. The empire of David and Solomon took its place among the empires of the earth.

The key figure in this period of Israel's history is David. He was the most outstanding man of his age. Through his leadership Israel was rescued from defeat and established in the land. David is significant also as a man of faith. He appears a thousand years before the coming of Christ. He reveals in his words and deeds a faith in the God of Israel which is meaningful both for the life of Israel and for the faith of all mankind. He consistently points beyond himself to the God who raised him up. As we live with him, we find that we cannot understand him apart from his encounter with the Lord. And through his revelation of himself to David in mercy and in judgment the Lord continues to confront us in the context of our life today.

David does not stand alone. There emerged during his time a group of men and women who were unique in the life of Israel. In fact, it would be hard to find either in literature or in history a more arresting aggregation of people than we find in the personalities around David. There were in his army men like the sons of Zeruiah—Joab, Abishai, and Asahel—and like Uriah the Hittite, Benaiah the son of Jehoiada, and the three mighty men who broke through the ranks of the Philistines to get David a drink of water from the well of Bethlehem. The world in which David lived was a rough and ready world dominated by men. But who would think of David without thinking of Merab and Michal, the daughters of Saul; of Abigail and the romance in the wilderness; of the beautiful Bathsheba; of Tamar, the daughter of David; and of the ministry to David performed by Abishag, the Shunammite.

As the background of the story of David we meet the men of the house of Saul: Saul himself a commanding and a tragic figure, Jonathan his son and the friend of David, the weak Ishbosheth, and Abner, a prince and a great man in Israel. Closely associated with the story of David are prophets like Samuel who anoints him, Nathan who rebukes him, Gad who advises him, and at the end Abijah who pronounces judgment on the house of David because of the sins of Solomon. As we live with David we meet priests such as Ahimelech at Nob, Abiathar his son, Zadok the priest who serves with Abiathar, and the sons of the priests, Ahimaaz and Jonathan.

In David's conflicts with the Philistines, we get glimpses of the men of the Philistines such as Achish, the king of the Philistine city of Gath; Goliath, the giant from Gath; and Ishbibenob, the giant who underestimated Abishai.

As the story of David moves on we meet the sons of David— Amnon his firstborn; Absalom, handsome but ambitious, scheming, and selfish; Adonijah, who thinks the kingdom belongs to him; and Solomon in all his glory and his weakness.

In the unfolding of this story we meet wise men like Ahithophel and Hushai and kings like Hiram of Tyre and Hanun the king of the Ammonites. The life of David's world stands revealed in the characters of the people around him.

The people who touch David's life are not the brilliant creations of a great writer. They are men and women who lived and loved and fought and died in the land of Palestine about three thousand years ago. Through them we have an intimate look into the life of the people of Israel at a crucial time in their history. We see them in their fears, their prejudices, their hates, and their loves. We see them most significantly of all in their worship, in their faith in the Lord, and in their consciousness of encounter with the Lord their God.

David and those around him are not the creations of a writer of fiction. No one questions their actual existence in Palestine about a thousand years before Christ. But our knowledge of David and those who stood around him has come to us from written materials preserved for us in the Old Testament. We do not know the writers of the documents which tell us the story of the age of David. We do know that we have preserved here some great writing. And scholars are generally agreed that the basic documents which give us the story of David were written at a time that was contemporaneous or almost so with the age of David. In particular we have a great throne-succession piece that tells the story of Absalom's rebellion. This document must have been written not long after the time of the events which it describes. Of course the stories concerning David were worked over and edited by later hands. But this does not change the fact that we have here very ancient documents which reflect the point of view of those who actually lived in the time of which they wrote.

There is a limited emphasis on the supernatural in the stories that come to us from the time of David, but the supernatural is present in these stories. We find it, for example, in the account of the calling up of Samuel by the witch of Endor (1 Samuel 28:3-25). It is present also in the story of the destroying angel at the time of the census and the plague (2 Samuel 24). But the judgments of God which took place in the experiences of David and those around him were not supernatural judgments. They came to pass in the context of their earthly life. David's failure in his personal life led to his failure to control either his home or his kingdom. And the judgments predicted by Nathan in the matter of Uriah the Hittite took place without any supernatural intervention. In these stories we see the Lord ruling and over-ruling in the midst of the passions of men and making the wrath of men to praise him. Who would have thought that David's punishment would come through the son he loved or that Abner in his affair with Rizpah would become the instrument of David's being established as king of all Israel?

While the judgments of God move in the context of our earthly life, in the stories of David we are confronted at every turn with the fact of the word of the Lord. The stories preserved here bear consistent witness to the coming of the word of the Lord. Samuel is the bearer of the word of the Lord's rejection to Saul. David is anointed by Samuel at the command of the Lord. David inquires of the Lord through Abiathar the priest at various crises in his life as a fugitive and in his decisions as king of Israel. After his sin with Bathsheba, the word of the Lord comes to David through the prophet Nathan. The prophet Gad is the bearer of the word of the Lord at the time of the census. The stories of David cannot be understood apart from the acceptance of the concept of the word of the Lord.

What is the relevance of the study of the stories of David and those around him for those who live in the modern world? Three thousand years of history separate us from David. David and his men moved in a simple pastoral and agricultural society. In the context of their lives in the Palestine of 1000 B.C. they appear to have little in common with the life of man in our complex industrial society. But there is an abiding human element in life which breaks through in spite of the changes in life situations. Who would fail to be moved by the story of the friendship between Jonathan and David? Who would find uninteresting the account of the death of Asahel at the hands of Abner and of the way in which Joab and Abishai thought that they must be the avengers of their brother's blood? The story of David in his sin moves where men live today. He becomes guilty of adultery with Bathsheba, and his sin with Bathsheba leads to the effort to cover his sin and to the tangled web that men weave when first they practice to deceive. Who can ever forget the picture of David as he waits for the report of the battle and for news of the fate of the young man Absalom? Through the stories of David and those around him we have a mirror of life that will continue to be relevant to every age.

And there is a dimension of depth in the stories of David that is not found in ordinary writings. A great dramatist can present with marvelous skill men and women in their interplay with each other. But the writer of the Old Testament narratives concerning David is primarily concerned with presenting people in their encounters with the Lord. It is because these accounts point to the Lord in his acts of judgment and mercy that they have abiding value for us.

In the study of the personalities around David, we will find many cases in which the word of the Lord spoken to an individual in his life situation can become the word of the Lord to us in our life situation. There is a word for us in the story of what Amnon did to himself when he failed to control his lust for his sister Tamar. The spiritual victory of Jonathan over the things that life brought to him will continue to be a challenge to all who follow after him. The dilemma of Ahithophel has something to say to every man who is tempted to put expediency above an absolute loyalty. There are other times in which the characters around David create a setting in which David is forced to give expression to his own faith. The argument between David and Abishai as they stand over the sleeping Saul is a life situation in which David must express his unwillingness to lift his hand against the Lord's anointed and his confidence that in time the Lord will establish him in the kingdom. The appearance of Goliath is the supreme test of David's conviction that the battle is the Lord's.

David and those who stand around him are of the earth, earthy. They do not see human life in the light of the revelation of God which has come to us in Jesus Christ. They show little interest in the life beyond the grave. (The one exception to this is David's hope of being reunited with his infant son.) They are concerned with the judgments of God that take place within the context of our earthly life. But they do speak to us of the way in which the word of the Lord came to them in their life situations. They point beyond themselves to the Lord their God, the God of Israel and the God of every human being.

# 2

## SAUL—anointed of the Lord but disobedient to the word of the Lord

*Scripture Background—1 Samuel 15*

"Behold, to obey is better than sacrifice . . .
Because you have rejected the word of the LORD, he has also rejected you from being king" (1 Samuel 15:22-23).

The story of the rejection of Saul holds our interest and at the same time gives us some genuine concern for an understanding of its meaning. The scene in which Samuel confronts Saul in the name of the Lord is a brilliant example of a dramatic narrative. And the knowledge that the Lord has rejected Saul as king of Israel is the key to the understanding of the stories that follow.

One question raised by this narrative is whether the God who has made himself known in Jesus Christ could have commanded the destruction of the Amalekites. We must remember that this story is set in the life of Palestine a thousand years before the coming of the Christ. We should remember also that a clear distinction must be made between action that is appropriate to God as the moral judge of the universe and conduct that is appropriate to us as individuals. Later in the history of Israel, God uses the armies of Assyria and Babylon as the instruments of his judgment against sinning Israel. Could he not in the same way have used the armies of Israel as the instruments of his judgment against the Amalekites when in his decision their cup of iniquity was full? In the New Testament as in the Old, we have the concept of the wrath of God. In one of the great passages of the

New Testament, Paul says to the Roman Christians: "Beloved, never avenge yourselves, but leave it to the wrath of God; for it is written, 'Vengeance is mine, I will repay, says the Lord' " (Romans 12:19). The Christian concept of love of enemies can be combined with the understanding that God as the vindicator of the moral order must move in judgment against those who persist in the way of evil.

The Amalekites were a robber tribe of desert warriors who lived by preying on their more peaceful neighbors. In the history of Israel we meet them first as they attack the Israelites immediately after their escape from Egypt by the crossing of the Red Sea. The first battle of Israel as a nation was fought with Amalek at Rephidim (Exodus 17:8-16). Among the last of the references to the Amalekites in Scripture is the story of their attack on Ziklag when David and his men had marched with the Philistines to the battle against Israel at Mount Gilboa. At this time the Amalekites burned the city with fire and carried the women and children into slavery. It was only by swift pursuit that David and his men were able to rescue their wives and children. When the Bible says, "The LORD will have war with Amalek from generation to generation" (Exodus 17:16), it expresses the eternal hostility of God to a people who live by plunder and pillage.

The children of Israel in the time of Saul were a scattered group of tribes held together by their common worship of the Lord. They were insecurely based in Palestine. The major threat to their continued existence as a people was the Philistine invasion from the south. But they were constantly exposed also to marauding tribes from the desert. Saul's first act as king was to gather together Israel and Judah for the deliverance of the people of Jabesh-gilead from the cruelty of Nahash, the Ammonite. The establishment of Israel as a kingdom required both the breaking of the power of the Philistines and the subjugation of the desert tribes to the east.

Saul was the first king of Israel. He had been made king in response to the demand of the people for a king to lead them against their enemies. He had been selected by a lot which the

Lord directed, and he had been anointed with oil by Samuel as the symbol of the divine appointment. He was known as the Lord's anointed. The expression is identical with that which later came to express the hope of a Messiah raised up by God for the deliverance of his people. As the king in a theocracy, Saul was expected to be obedient to the word of the Lord. As the Lord's anointed he was to be the instrument of the divine purpose.

The command to Saul was to destroy Amalek utterly. It was clear that Saul and his people were not to seize any of the spoil of the Amalekites for themselves. The Israelites were not to enrich themselves by victory. The destruction of Amalek was to stand out before the ancient world as an act of divine judgment even as the destruction of Sodom and Gomorrah had made a profound impression on the world of Abraham.

It is in this setting that we must understand the failure of Saul. In his sparing of Agag and in his saving alive of the best of the sheep and oxen, Saul is not moved by humanitarian motives. The motive for his disobedience is first of all greed. The Israelites wanted the spoil for themselves. Saul is moved also by pride. He wants to display the captured king in triumph on his return. He may have been motivated somewhat by fear of the people, but it is likely that Saul and the people were in agreement in their determination to keep the spoil for themselves. We should notice also that the disobedience of Saul is the beginning of stubbornness. He soon moves on to such morally indefensible acts as the destruction of the priests of the Lord and the plunder of the Gibeonites in violation of a sacred treaty. Saul does not know the meaning of genuine repentance. He says, "I have sinned," more frequently than any other character in the Bible. But his real concern in this incident is not that he has disobeyed the Lord but his desire not to lose face before the people by failing to worship the Lord along with Samuel.

The disobedience of Saul turned an expedition which should have stood out before the world as an act of divine judgment into an expedition that must have looked to the rest of the world very much like a raid for spoil. In this the Israelites were

on a moral plane which was little better than that of the Amalekites. The note of divine judgment was lost in the greed of the
Israelites.

Saul is a tragic figure. He was a man of great possibilities, but
his disobedience to the word of the Lord was the fatal flaw
which made it impossible for him to be adequate to the task to
which he was called.

When confronted by Samuel in the name of the Lord, Saul
sought to put the blame on the people and to cover up the act
of disobedience by saying that the people saved alive the best of
the flocks and herds to sacrifice unto the Lord in Gilgal. This
gives the setting for Samuel's statement:

> "Has the LORD as great delight in burnt offerings and sacrifices,
>     as in obeying the voice of the LORD?
> Behold, to obey is better than sacrifice,
>     and to hearken than the fat of rams.
> For rebellion is as the sin of divination,
>     and stubbornness is as iniquity and idolatry.
> Because you have rejected the word of the LORD,
>     he has also rejected you from being king."

In this utterance, Samuel rises to the prophetic insight that the
condition of the heart is more important in the sight of God than
the observance of the forms and ceremonies of religion. In God's
demand upon Saul there was to be no substitute for obedience
to the word of the Lord. Rebellion is as the sin of divination, in
which a man puts his own will against the will of God. Stubbornness is as idolatry, in which a man substitutes a false god for the
God who has made himself known through his word. In Saul's
refusal to be obedient to the word of the Lord he has revealed
himself as unfit to be the instrument of the divine purpose. He
is rejected as king because he has rejected the word of the Lord.
The rejection of Saul prepares the way for the appearance of
David, the man whom the Lord has chosen to become king of
Israel.

The message spoken to Saul is relevant in the life of the
modern world. The forms and ceremonies of religion cannot be
substituted for the heart that responds in love and obedience to

the revelation that God has made of himself. We today are not tempted to cover our disobedience with a multitude of animal sacrifices. But we can be tempted to substitute a parade of the forms of religion for readiness to be obedient to the will of God. The Ten Commandments are given to be obeyed. A program of activities at the church is not a substitute for obedience to the moral law. Jesus himself has said to us: "Not every one who *says* to me, 'Lord, Lord,' shall enter the kingdom of heaven, but he who *does* the will of my Father who is in heaven" (Matthew 7:21). He has also said: "If you love me, you will keep my commandments"(John 14:15).

From the study of the man who was the first to be called "The Lord's anointed" but who revealed himself as disobedient to the word of the Lord and was rejected as king, we turn to the figure of the Christ who was also called the Lord's Anointed. The writer to the Hebrews pictures the Christ as saying to the Father:

> "Sacrifices and offerings thou hast not desired . . .
> in burnt offerings and sin offerings thou hast
>     taken no pleasure.
> Then I said, 'Lo, I have come to do thy will, O God' "
>     (Hebrews 10:5-7).

The Christ faced the inadequacy of sacrifices either to please God as a substitute for obedience or to atone for the sins of disobedience. In the knowledge of the inadequacy of all other sacrifices he offered himself as the one who had come to do the will of God even if this led to the cross. In so doing he became the Anointed of the Lord who in the time of testing remained obedient to the will of God.

# 3

## SAMUEL—who anointed David as king

*Scripture Background—1 Samuel 16:1-13*

"The LORD sees not as man sees; man looks on the outward appearance, but the LORD looks on the heart" (1 Samuel 16:7).

As we read the story of Samuel's anointing of David, we are impressed by the divine initiative in this story. It is the Lord who has found among the sons of Jesse a man with the capacity to become king of Israel. Samuel is called away from his mourning for Saul to undertake a mission which he enters upon in obedience to the command of the Lord. The Lord rejects seven of the sons of Jesse, then David is anointed after the Lord says to Samuel: "Arise, anoint him; for this is he." Following the anointing, the Spirit of the Lord comes mightily upon David.

This is among the last of the stories that we have in the life of Samuel. Others, of course, tell of David's flight to Samuel at Ramah (1 Samuel 19:18-24), and of Samuel's appearance before Saul when called up by the medium at Endor (1 Samuel 28). But evidently Samuel no longer had an active part in the life of Israel. In his anointing of David, Samuel appeared, as in the other stories, as the bearer of the word of the Lord.

We are told that preceding the appearance of Samuel, "the word of the LORD was rare in those days; there was no frequent vision" (1 Samuel 3:1). The first recorded incident in the life of Samuel is the story of the way in which the word of the Lord came to him while he was a boy ministering to the Lord under Eli. The young Samuel faithfully delivered to the aged Eli the word of the Lord that came as a judgment on Eli and his sons.

We are dealing here with the concept of the word of the Lord. It is the phenomenon in which the Lord speaks to individuals at times of his own choosing, imparting information and giving them a word of command.

We have here also the concept of "the anointed of the Lord." The anointing of a person with oil in obedience to the word of the Lord was a ceremony which recognized God's calling of a specific person to a particular work. Aaron was anointed with oil when he was consecrated as high priest (Exodus 29:7, 21). Saul was anointed with oil by Samuel when he was chosen by the Lord to be prince over his people Israel (1 Samuel 10:1). David in his lament over Saul remembers the former glory of Saul and grieves that his fate is "as though he had not been anointed with oil" (2 Samuel 1:21, K.J.V.). We should remember that the word "Messiah" means anointed and that the Greek translation of this word is *Christ*. It was against the background of the Old Testament understanding of the Lord's anointed that there was developed in the history of Israel the concept of the Messiah as the one whom the Lord would raise up to deliver his people. This idea finds its fulfillment in Jesus, the Christ.

It is in the story we are considering that the Scripture gives us our introduction to David. David is not the major actor in this story. He comes at the end of the story as the son of Jesse whom the Lord had selected to be king. The Lord has looked into his heart and found the man he is seeking. David comes to us as a boy in his late teens. He is tanned by the sun, and he has the vigorous health of one who has lived an outdoor life. He has beautiful eyes through which we look into a sensitive soul. He is handsome. In his native endowment he is one of the most gifted men of Israel's history. He has the capacity to become a great leader of men in battle. He is gifted in music and is destined to become the sweet psalmist of Israel. Through his expressions of his own faith in the Lord, he has spoken to the spiritual needs of the people of God in all ages. But in this story we meet him as the boy who is called from his keeping of the sheep. He has been selected as the Lord's anointed because of what the Lord has seen in his heart.

As an integral part of this story there is spoken to Samuel a word of the Lord that had meaning in the setting in which it was spoken and continues to speak to us today. When Samuel looks at Eliab, the first of the sons of Jesse to pass before him, he thinks: "Surely the LORD's anointed is before him." He does not say "before *me*." He knows that the Lord's anointed must stand before the Lord. But the Lord says to Samuel: "Do not look on his appearance or on the height of his stature, because I have rejected him; for the LORD sees not as man sees; man looks on the outward appearance, but the LORD looks on the heart" (1 Samuel 16:7). Samuel has seen the height of Eliab's stature and the beauty of his countenance, but the Lord has looked into Eliab's heart and rejected him. The choice of David is a tribute to the young David as a man after God's own heart.

There is no criticism of Samuel involved in the statement "man looks on the outward appearance." This is what man sees first. We judge people by their outward appearance. We look for beauty in women and strength in men. We study the lines in people's faces and make our estimates of their age. We see their clothes and form our opinion concerning the money they spend on clothes or their taste in dress.

Because man looks on the outward appearance, we seek to present an image of ourselves to the eyes of men. The other side of this procedure is that as we look on the outward appearance we seek to go behind it to a true knowledge of the inner life. Absalom, a son of David, was without flaw in his physical appearance. And Absalom built up in the minds of the people of Israel an image of himself as a king who would serve their interests. But in time he revealed himself as a son who would seek to take the life of his father to satisfy his own ambitions.

Man looks on the outward appearance. But men learn also to look behind the outward appearance to the things that reveal the real person. There will always be an unguarded moment in which the man who lives behind a mask will make himself known. We do not know why Eliab was rejected, but we do know that if he had been thrust into positions of trust and responsibility the flaw in him would in time have been revealed. As we deal with people it is far better for us to be genuine than for us to seek to build in others an image of ourselves that does not correspond with what we are.

The deepest thrust of the word of the Lord to Samuel is in the statement "The LORD looks on the heart." Although we can present to men an outward appearance that does not correspond with what we are, we cannot deceive the Lord for one moment.

Yet we must not think of God merely in terms of an all-seeing eye that penetrates always to the inmost recesses of our being. The God whom Jesus has revealed to us is the loving and compassionate Father who calls us to become his children. As the disciples thought of God they recalled Jesus' teaching and said, "This is the message we have heard from him and proclaim to you, that God is light and in him is no darkness at all" (1 John 1:5). God is the loving Father who never deceives and whom we can never deceive. Because of what he is, God calls us to walk in the light as he is in the light. And if we walk in the light as he is in the light, there are two things that follow. The first is that we have fellowship with one another (1 John 1:7). We enter into real fellowship with each other when we come out from behind our masks and reveal ourselves to each other as we really are. And when we confess our sins and put away all hypocrisy and pretense, the blood of Jesus the Son of God cleanses us from all sin (1 John 1:7). When we have received this cleansing, we do not need to be afraid when God looks into our hearts. It was David who, when he had sinned greatly, came at last to the understanding that God desires truth in the inward being (Psalm 51:6). And then he was able to pray: "Create in me a clean heart, O God, and put a new and right spirit within me" (Psalm 51:10).

# 4

## GOLIATH—who defied "the armies of the living God"

*Scripture Background: 1 Samuel 17*

"The battle is the LORD's" (1 Samuel 17:47).

The encounter of David with Goliath of Gath created a situation in which David expressed his conviction that the battle is the Lord's. Even those who do not share this faith must respect it when they realize that it was in the strength of this conviction that David went forth to do battle with the Philistine giant.

In the time of David, the Philistines constituted the most serious threat that Israel had faced in Palestine. The Philistines had entered Palestine by the sea and had firmly established themselves as a group of city-states located in the rich coastal plain to the south and west of Judah. They had forced the tribe of Dan to migrate to the north to escape destruction. When David was keeping his sheep in the hills around Bethlehem, the Philistines were preparing for the conquest of all of Palestine. The history of nations can be interpreted in terms of stimulus and response. It was the response of Israel to the Philistine threat that forced the formation of the Hebrew monarchy.

When Goliath defied the armies of Israel he became a symbol of the threat of the Philistines to the continued existence of Israel as the people of the Lord. As Goliath issues his challenge, he takes his place in the long line of those who in their arrogance have thought that they could defy the God who has made himself known in Israel. And when David goes out to battle with Goliath he does not go as a daring young man in search of personal glory. He goes because he feels that the honor of the Lord is at stake. He is concerned that all the earth may know that there is a God in Israel.

We must not underestimate the David who dared to accept the challenge of Goliath and fight for Israel. Sometime before this David had been anointed with oil by Samuel. He knew himself as the Lord's anointed, and he must have felt that the call he had received through Samuel involved the readiness to enter into combat with those who defied the armies of the Lord.

The David who confronts Goliath stands on the threshold of manhood. He has been hardened by his outdoor life as the shepherd of his father's sheep. In his life as a shepherd he has fought and killed first a lion and then a bear. He is a master in the use of the sling—a deadly weapon in the hands of those who know how to handle it. Michaelangelo's famous statue of David is his conception of the young David as sling in hand he goes out to the battle. He has given us the figure of a young man in his strength.

When David in response to Goliath's taunts cries out that the battle is the Lord's he is expressing a faith that was not unique in Israel. David believed that in the day of battle the Lord was present overruling the actions of men and determining the outcome of the conflict.

In this David does not stand in isolation from other leaders of Israel. This faith is expressed in dramatic form in the story of Gideon and the deliverance from Midian which the Lord wrought through him. Gideon was directed to reduce his army to three hundred men in order that all men might know that the victory over Midian was of the Lord (Judges 7:2-8). The same faith is expressed by Jonathan at Michmash when he says to the young man who bears his armor: "Come, let us go over to the garrison of these uncircumcised; it may be that the LORD will work for us; for nothing can hinder the LORD from saving by many or by few" (1 Samuel 14:6). As an expression of this faith Jonathan and his armor-bearer began an attack against seemingly hopeless odds, and the Lord worked through them to give victory to Israel. The same faith is expressed by Joab when in the war with the Ammonites he finds himself suddenly confronted by the Ammonites attacking from the city of Rabbah and the Syrians unexpectedly attacking from the other side. In this situation Joab says to his men: "Be of good courage, and let us play the man for our people, and for the cities of our God; and may the LORD do what seems good to him" (2 Samuel 10:12). Joab knew that he and his soldiers must do their part, but he knew also that the final decision concerning the outcome of the battle was with the Lord.

The faith of the captains of Israel's armies was also the faith of her great prophets. When Isaiah faced the armies of Assyria as they marched triumphantly into Palestine, his faith in the power of the Lord would not permit him for one moment to believe that the Assyrians were victorious because the Lord was unable to stop them. Instead he saw the Assyrians as the rod of the Lord's anger and the staff of his fury (Isaiah 10:5). He knew that in the end the Lord would punish "the arrogant boasting of the king of Assyria" (Isaiah 10:12). In a similar manner Jeremiah interpreted the destruction of Jerusalem by the king of Babylon as the expression of the judgment of the Lord on a sinful people.

In a very different situation Jesus gave expression to the same faith in the power of God. When the soldiers of the chief priests seized Jesus, Peter drew his sword. He struck a blow in which he cut off the ear of the servant of the high priest. But Jesus said to him: "Put your sword back into its place; for all who take the sword will perish by the sword. Do you think that I cannot appeal to my Father, and he will at once send me more than twelve legions of angels? But how then should the scriptures be fulfilled, that it must be so?" (Matthew 26:52-54). Jesus knew that in the will of his Father it was necessary for him to suffer and die to accomplish his work. But he never doubted for a moment the power of God to intervene effectively for his deliverance.

The belief that the battle is the Lord's is never an obvious understanding of history. The secular historian would say that in the day of battle victory usually comes to the side that has the biggest battalions. And we can find many things in the course of history to support his position. Again and again in the history of mankind the small but righteous nation has gone down in defeat before a powerful and ruthless aggressor. The conviction that the Lord determines the outcome of the battle is a penetrating insight into the meaning of history which is held by those who have the knowledge of God that has come by revelation. It was because of their knowledge of the mighty acts of God in the events of Israel's history that the children of Israel were convinced that the battle was the Lord's. It was because they could not repudiate their heritage that they continued to hold this faith even when it did not seem to fit in with the events of their contemporary history. And it was because the first Christians had seen the risen Lord that they were convinced that all power had been given to him in heaven and in earth.

The belief that the battle is the Lord's grows out of the conviction that God is sovereign. David and those who stood with him were confident that the Lord was able to rule and overrule in the affairs of men. They believed in a God who was able to make the wrath of man to praise him. If we were to translate their faith into the contemporary scene we would say that the ultimate decisions of history are made not in Washington or Moscow but by God himself. In the midst of the tensions of our times we need to believe in a God who is sovereign. Our generation lives in the constant threat of wholesale destruction through the use of atomic weapons. In the crisis of our time we should remember that God is sovereign and that this day of destruction will not come unless God permits it as a judgment on a civilization that has forgotten him.

The belief that the battle is the Lord's did not cause the Israelites to lose their sense of personal responsibility. David leaves the outcome of the conflict with Goliath in the hands of the Lord, but he goes out to fight effectively with the weapon he knows how to handle. Joab tells his men to be of good courage and to play the man in the day of the battle with the Syrians. He leaves the issue of the battle to the Lord, but he leads the charge against the Syrians.

When men believe that the battle is the Lord's it does not always follow that victory will come to those who are sure they are fighting the battles of the Lord. Jonathan was confident that it was the will of the Lord for the Israelites to prevail over the Philistines in the struggle for the mastery of Canaan. And Jonathan at Michmash led the attack on the Philistines in the confidence that the Lord could save by many or by few. His faith was vindicated in the outcome of the battle. But a few years later Jonathan was fighting on Mount Gilboa. He had shot his last arrow. His bow was useless. Saul, his father, had fallen on his sword to avoid capture at the hands of the Philistines. His men had fled and the Philistines were coming on. This was not the day for Israel to win. But the death of Jonathan at the hand of the Philistines did not mean that the Lord had ceased to be the One who determines the outcome of the battle. We cannot always be sure of the will of God in the particular struggle in which we are engaged. But we can be sure that God will remain sovereign and that in ways we may not understand he is accomplishing his purposes.

If we believe that the outcome of the struggle is in the hands of God it is important for us to seek to do the will of God. The God who has made himself known to us in Jesus Christ is a God of infinite compassion. He is also a God of holiness. He is unalterably opposed to the sin and evil of our world. It is proper for the people of a nation to prepare to defend themselves against aggression from without. It is necessary for a people to use police power to maintain order within the life of the nation. But a nation makes a basic mistake when it puts its trust in military power rather than in righteousness.

We cannot bring God into the battle on our terms. We must seek to serve him if we expect him to give victory to us in the great conflicts of our time. We cannot expect the blessing of God on our society if we fail to use our strength to seek to establish justice in the earth. The children of Israel knew that they had to walk the road of repentance and obedience if they were to be able to hope that the Lord would give victory to their armies in the day of battle. The nation that forgets God will perish either through inward decay or through foreign invasion. And the nations that seek to know and serve the purposes of God in the earth will come to know that the Lord is their "refuge and strength, a very present help in trouble" (Psalm 46:1).

# 5

## JONATHAN—son of Saul and friend of David

*Scripture Background: 1 Samuel 14; 18:1-5; 19:1-7; 20; 23:15-18; 31; 2 Samuel 1:17-27*

"The bow of Jonathan turned not back" (2 Samuel 1:22).

When David said of Jonathan, "The bow of Jonathan turned not back," he was thinking of Jonathan as a man mighty in battle and in particular of a man skilled in the use of the bow as a weapon of war. But we do not distort the words when we think of them as expressing the spirit of a man who faced with courage and faith the difficult things which life brought to him— of a man who, as expressed in Browning's *Asolando,* "never turned his back but marched breast forward."

From the beginning of the reign of Saul, Jonathan fought with his father in the wars with the Philistines and in the wars with the nations around about Israel. When Saul gathered together the first standing army in Israel, he himself assumed command of a company of two thousand men and placed Jonathan in command of a thousand men (1 Samuel 13:2-4). It is as a part of the record of the battles of Saul with the Philistines that we have the account of the attack of Jonathan and his armor-bearer on a garrison of the Philistines at Michmash (1 Samuel 14). This story reveals the courage of Jonathan and his skill as a mighty man of valor. Jonathan initiated an attack which in the end turned the tide of battle and resulted in victory for Israel. The story is interesting also for the picture it gives us of Jonathan as a man of faith in God. It is here that Jonathan says to his armor-bearer: "Come, let us go over to the garrison of these uncircumcised; it may be that the LORD will work for us; for nothing can hinder the LORD from saving by many or by few" (1 Samuel 14:6). Jonathan has this faith and acts upon it, and the Lord is with him in the day of battle to give him victory over seemingly impossible odds. This saying of Jonathan's should be set alongside of David's "The battle is the LORD's" as affirmations of Israel's faith in the Lord as the God of battles.

The picture which we have of Jonathan would indicate that he was well fitted to follow his father on the throne of Israel. But the time came when Saul was rejected by the Lord as king of Israel. Saul's rejection was based upon his disobedience to the word of the Lord. The rejection of Saul included the rejection of his house. It meant that Jonathan would not follow his father as the second of Israel's kings. And as it became known that David had been anointed with oil by Samuel in obedience to the command of the Lord (1 Samuel 16:13), it became clear that it was the will of the Lord for the throne to go to David.

Jonathan's reaction to this word of the Lord was probably the crucial decision of his life. Saul refused to accept the word of the Lord. He became insanely jealous of David and neglected his duties as king to concentrate on the attempt to destroy him. As he did this he deteriorated in character and performed deeds of shame, such as the slaughter of the priests at Nob, that weakened him and alienated his people. Jonathan in contrast to his father accepted the word of the Lord. He was ready to take second place if this was the will of the Lord. He expressed this in the vivid scene in which he placed his robe on David and gave him his armor, his sword, his bow, and his girdle (1 Samuel 18:1-5). Jonathan did more than this. He made David his intimate friend. We are told that the soul of Jonathan was knit to the soul of David and that Jonathan loved him as his own soul. We have therefore a strange situation in which Saul seeks to kill David in order that Jonathan may be king and Jonathan can say to David: "You shall be king over Israel, and I shall be next to you; Saul my father also knows this" (1 Samuel 23:17).

Dean Stanley has described the friendship of David and Jona-

than as an attachment "which is the first Biblical instance of a
romantic friendship . . . and is remarkable, both as giving its
sanction to these, and as filled with a pathos of its own, which
has been imitated but never surpassed, in modern works of
fiction. Each found in each the affection that he had not found
in his own family."

In his lament over Saul and Jonathan, David says:

> "Jonathan lies slain upon thy high places.
> I am distressed for you, my brother Jonathan;
> very pleasant have you been to me;
> your love to me was wonderful,
> passing the love of women" (2 Samuel 1:25-26).

The friendship of David and Jonathan points out the costliness
of great friendship. Who can know the struggle that must have
gone on in the soul of Jonathan as he accepted the idea that
David was to be king and that the most he could hope for was to
be next to David. We can be sure that this was one instance
of Jonathan's encounter with God and of Jonathan's acceptance of
the word of the Lord.

The friendship of David and Jonathan does give its sanction
to a strong friendship between two men or to a similar friendship
between two women. Such relationships have in them elements
of danger. They can become so exclusive that they limit the
capacity for forming other friendships. But they can become
also deep and enriching experiences that help to give meaning to
life. We have no reason to think that the friendship of David
and Jonathan was exclusive or narrowing. The friendship of David
and Jonathan will continue to stand out in history as an example
of a great and noble friendship.

In his friendship with David, Jonathan found that his loyalty
to his father was tested. Jonathan refused to join his father in
his jealousy of David or to have any part in his father's determination to kill David. Even when David was fleeing from Saul,
Jonathan sought out David in the wilderness and spoke with
him. But Jonathan remained loyal to his father. David could
write of them: "Saul and Jonathan were lovely and pleasant in

their lives, and in their death they were not divided" (2 Samuel 1:23, K.J.V.).

Jonathan stayed with his father to the end. He marched with Saul to the fatal battle on Mount Gilboa. But he had no part in Saul's turning to the witch of Endor. Jonathan entered a battle in which it looked as if David would be fighting with the Philistines against the army of Israel. We wonder what would have happened if David and Jonathan had met in battle. But they were spared this by the well-grounded fears of the leaders of the Philistines when they insisted that David and his men should not be permitted to go into the battle against Israel.

Jonathan perished in that battle. He did not take his own life as Saul did when he saw that the battle was lost. He died at the hands of the Philistines, but it was not until the day after the battle that the Philistines knew that Jonathan was among the slain. He perished in a battle the loss of which seemed at the time to be fatal to the cause of Israel. The Philistine armies swept over his home. Of his children only his youngest son, Mephibosheth, escaped, and he was dropped by the fleeing nurse and injured so that he was left a cripple for life. Jonathan did not live to see the establishment of the kingdom in its strength, with the Philistines driven back to their cities and with the nations around about Israel subdued or bound to Israel in ties of friendship. He did not live to stand next to David when he became king.

Saul and Jonathan perished on Mount Gilboa. In death as in life they were not divided. But Saul came to his death as one of the most tragic figures in Israel. He had possibilities of real greatness. But in his rejection of the word of the Lord and in his jealousy of David he disintegrated until at the time of his death he was but a shadow of the man he might have been. Jonathan in his death is not a tragic figure. In his acceptance of the word of the Lord and in his friendship with David he rose triumphant over the difficult things he had to face. The real measure of a man is not in terms of success or failure but in terms of what he does with the things life brings him.

Ernest Gordon, in his *Through the Valley of the Kwai*, tells the story of two men who were his companions in the prison

camp in the valley of the Kwai. They were Dinty Moore and
Dusty Miller. These two men were used of God in a most remarkable way to stop the process of disintegration that was
going on among the prisoners. They met hate with love. They
gave themselves in a loving ministry to those who were around
them. They bore witness to the Christ as a man who was also
a man of sorrows and acquainted with grief. They played a
major part in the movement through which the reality of the
Christian church became evident in the midst of a community of
desperate, dying men. They helped to set in motion redemptive
forces which are still at work in our world.

We wish we could say that at the end of the war these men
emerged as survivors of the ordeal of suffering and as obviously
reaping the fruits of their spiritual ministry. But the facts are
that Dinty Moore perished in a boat, loaded with prisoners of
war, that was torpedoed by a submarine just a short time before
the war was over, and Dusty Miller was brutally put to death by
a guard who could not understand a man who was spiritually
victorious over hate and suffering. Life is often like that. Paul has
told us not to be weary in welldoing "for in due season we shall
reap, if we do not lose heart" (Galatians 6:9). But we do not
always see the day of reaping. When we look at life in the
dimensions of the Christian faith we know that the final judgment of life must be seen in the light of our knowledge of the
resurrection life of God which lies beyond death. This is true
of Dinty Moore and Dusty Miller. It is true also of Jonathan.
But even if we had no knowledge of the life that is beyond
death, we could say that the final measure of a man is his
spiritual victory over that which life brings him. No man can
determine the course he will have to run as he passes through
the pilgrimage of life. But those who believe in God can believe
that this course is set for them by the one who is the Creator
and Sustainer of all life. When the life of Jonathan is seen in
this pattern we know that his was a life of spiritual triumph.

# 6

## MEPHIBOSHETH—son of Jonathan and befriended by David

*Scripture Background: 1 Samuel 20; 23:15-18; 2 Samuel 4:4; 9; 16:1-4; 19:24-30; 21:7; 1 Chronicles 8:33-34*

"God remembered his covenant" (Exodus 2:24).

The story of Mephibosheth begins with the story of the covenant between David and Jonathan. In the days when David was serving as Saul's armor-bearer, there had grown up a deep friendship between Jonathan and David. This friendship continued in spite of Jonathan's knowledge of David's anointing and the expectancy that David rather than Jonathan would become king.

The covenant between the two men was made at a crucial time in the life of David. Saul's growing jealousy of David was well known, and a short while after his daughter Michal had been given to David as his wife, Saul sent soldiers to kill David in his home. David escaped and went to Samuel at Ramah. Saul followed him there, but David escaped again. After this he went to Jonathan and asked Jonathan to find out with certainty whether or not his death would come if he placed himself again in the hands of Saul. It is in this scene that Jonathan says to David: "When the LORD cuts off every one of the enemies of David from the face of the earth, let not the name of Jonathan be cut off from the house of David" (1 Samuel 20:14-16). We are told that "Jonathan made David swear again by his love for him; for he loved him as he loved his own soul" (1 Samuel 20:17).

Saul's intentions concerning David were made clear when the father in fury cast his javelin at his own son, and it was on the next day that Jonathan met David in the famous scene in which he gave the signal by shooting the arrows over the head of the boy who was to gather them. The friends knew that they must follow separate ways. Jonathan must return to his life with Saul while his heart was with David. And David must set out as a lonely wanderer who sought in vain to find refuge in the land of the Philistines. Before they parted Jonathan said to David: "Go in peace, forasmuch as we have sworn both of us in the name of the LORD, saying, 'The LORD shall be between me and you, and between my descendants and your descendants, for ever'" (1 Samuel 20:42).

So far as we know, Jonathan never saw David again except for one brief visit when Jonathan went to David "and strengthened his hand in God" while David and his men were hiding in the wilderness of Ziph. Jonathan said to David: "Fear not; for the hand of Saul my father shall not find you; you shall be king over Israel, and I shall be next to you; Saul my father also knows this" (1 Samuel 23:17). At the close of this meeting the covenant which had already been made was reaffirmed. "And the two of them made a covenant before the LORD; David remained at Horesh, and Jonathan went home" (1 Samuel 23: 18).

After David had spared Saul's life in the cave of Engedi, there was a temporary reconciliation between Saul and David. Saul said to David: "And now, behold, I know that you shall surely be king, and that the kingdom of Israel shall be established in your hand. Swear to me therefore by the LORD that you will not cut off my descendants after me, and that you will not destroy my name out of my father's house" (1 Samuel 24:20-21).

In the ancient world it was customary for the king of a new dynasty to put to death all the descendants of the former king in order not to leave any person who could become the center of revolt. But David agreed not to kill every man of the house of Saul. We are told that "David swore this to Saul," and the king returned to his home (1 Samuel 24:22).

Events moved rapidly after the final separation of David and Jonathan. David and his men sought the protection of the Philistines, and Jonathan met his death in the crushing defeat of the armies of Israel on Mount Gilboa. The depth of David's devotion to Jonathan is indicated in the closing lines of his elegy over Saul and Jonathan.

"Jonathan lies slain upon thy high places.
I am distressed for you, my brother Jonathan;
very pleasant have you been to me;
  your love to me was wonderful,
  passing the love of women" (2 Samuel 1:25–26).

We realize the full dimensions of the defeat of Israel when we learn that the victorious army of the Philistines swept over the whole of Israel on the west side of Jordan. They came to the home of Jonathan. Jonathan had a son named Mephibosheth, who was five years old at the time of the battle of Gilboa. His nurse fled with him, and in her haste she dropped him. As a result of this fall he was permanently lame in both his feet. We do not know how many children Jonathan had, but we do know that Mephibosheth was the only descendant of Jonathan to survive the battle of Gilboa.

Very little is known of the life of Mephibosheth in the years that followed. Abner with a remnant of Saul's army was able to set up a kingdom at Mahanaim on the east of Jordan, with Ishbosheth, Saul's only surviving son, as king (2 Samuel 2:8-10). Mephibosheth found refuge in the home of a man named Machir, the son of Ammiel, who lived at a place called Lo-debar, a village on the east side of Jordan that was in the same general area as Mahanaim. Machir must have been a man of some means. Many years later when David fled from Absalom, Machir was one of those who came bringing provisions for David and his army (2 Samuel 17:27-29).

In this spot which was far removed from the centers of Israel's life, Mephibosheth grew to manhood. As he was lame in both his feet, he was unable to enter into many of the normal activities of life. He could not work and was no longer in possession of the land that had been the heritage of his family, so he was dependent on the charity of others. In time he married and had a son whose name was Mica (2 Samuel 9:12). From 1 Chronicles 8:33-40, where Mephibosheth is called Merib-bael, we learn that Mica became the father of four sons. It was through this son of Mephibosheth that the line of Saul was perpetuated in Israel.

After David had established himself as king over all Israel, he remembered his covenant with Jonathan. When he inquired whether any of the descendants of Jonathan were living, he was told by a man named Ziba, a former servant of Saul, that Mephibosheth, the cripple, was all that was left of Jonathan's family. David immediately sent for Mephibosheth that he might show kindness to him for the sake of Jonathan. David restored to Mephibosheth the lands that had formerly been the ancestral inheritance of his grandfather Saul. David ordered Ziba to farm the land and to bring to Mephibosheth the landowner's portion. This gave to Mephibosheth and his family a dependable source of income. As far as Mephibosheth himself was concerned, David insisted that he should live at Jerusalem and be treated as one of the sons of the king.

As we evaluate David's action, we should remember that Mephibosheth was the son of Jonathan, the firstborn son of Saul. By birth he stood in line for the throne. But we must admit that the crippled Mephibosheth was not likely to ever become a serious threat to David in his position as king of Israel. We can hope that in time David came to love Mephibosheth and to show kindness to him for his own sake. But in the beginning David's kindness to him was not based on any qualities that he discovered in Mephibosheth. David showed kindness to Mephibosheth because he remembered the covenant he had made before the Lord with Jonathan.

David's kindness to Mephibosheth for Jonathan's sake was tested in two incidents. We do not know which of these came first, but we will deal first with Mephibosheth and the judgment on the house of Saul because of Saul's slaughter of the Gibeonites. The Gibeonites demanded that seven men of the house of Saul be turned over to them for punishment in expiation for Saul's destruction of many of their people. David reluctantly consented. There is no trace here of any desire on the part of David for vengeance on the house of Saul. He was moved solely by the desire to remove bloodguiltiness from Israel. (The men of the house of Saul may not have shared this conviction.) In this crisis, David protected Mephibosheth for Jonathan's sake. He refused to let Mephibosheth be among the seven men of the house of Saul turned over to the Gibeonites.

The relation between David and Mephibosheth was tested also at the time of Absalom's rebellion. Mephibosheth did not go with David into exile. He had to do some explaining when David returned in triumph (2 Samuel 16:1-4 and 19:24-30). We will leave it to the individual reader to decide whether Ziba or Mephibosheth is telling the truth in this incident. But the closing words of Mephibosheth have a ring of genuineness. If we accept them as the words of an honest man, we can know that in the heart of the son of Jonathan there was deep and genuine love for David.

In the story of David as he remembers his covenant with Jonathan and shows kindness to Mephibosheth for Jonathan's sake, we have on the human plane an inadequate illustration of the way in which God remembers his covenant and moves to deliver his people. In the story of the Exodus we have a description of the people of Israel as they groaned in their bondage and cried out for help. "Their cry under bondage came up to God. And God heard their groaning, and God remembered his covenant with Abraham, with Isaac, and with Jacob. And God saw the people of Israel, and God knew their condition" (Exodus 2:23-25). Here is a picture of God remembering his covenant with Abraham and moving to deliver his people.

When parents who are themselves members of the believing community of the people of God bring their infant children to the church to receive baptism, they claim for their children the same great covenant mercies of God that they have already claimed for themselves. They pray that the God who is their God and the God who has been the God of their parents will also be the God of their children. They commit their children to God in the prayer that their faith may become alive in the hearts of their children. They agree to bring their children up in the nurture and admonition of the Lord and in the hope that God will call their children to be a part of his covenant people. David remembered his covenant with Jonathan, and for Jonathan's sake he showed kindness to Jonathan's son, Mephibosheth. All human illustrations are imperfect and inadequate as we seek to understand the God who comes to us and calls us into covenant relation with himself. But we can know that we are dealing with the God who remembers the covenant made with Abraham and renewed with David and extended through Jesus Christ to all who will receive it. As David remembers his covenant with Jonathan and shows kindness to Mephibosheth, he reminds us of the God who enters into covenant with us to be our God and the God of our children after us.

# 7

## ABNER—captain of Saul's armies, a prince and a great man in Israel

*Scripture Background: 1 Samuel 14:49-51; 17:55-58; 26:13-16; 2 Samuel 2:8—4:3; 1 Chronicles 8:33; 9:39*

"God do so to Abner, and more also, if I do not accomplish for David what the LORD has sworn to him, to transfer the kingdom from the house of Saul, and set up the throne of David over Israel and over Judah, from Dan to Beer-sheba" (2 Samuel 3:9).

Abner was the captain of Saul's army. He is known as the son of Ner as Saul is known as the son of Kish. The probability is that Abner and Saul were first cousins, although the references in Chronicles would seem to indicate that Ner was Saul's grandfather and that Abner himself was Saul's uncle. We do know that for seven years after the death of Saul, Abner was a vigorous man who was capable of engaging actively in battle. As captain of the armies of Israel under Saul, Abner must have been deeply involved in Saul's battles with the Philistines and with the nations around about Israel. But we do not have any record of this part of Abner's life. We would judge that he was a brave and able commander of men but that as a military genius he would not be in the class with David or Joab.

The probability is that Abner's first contact with David was when he stood with Saul and watched the young David go out to do battle with the Philistine, Goliath of Gath (1 Samuel 17:55-58). As captain of the army of Saul, Abner must have been closely associated with David during the time when David as an officer in Saul's army was actually assuming the responsibility of leading the Israelites into battle. When the representatives of the tribes of Israel came to David at Hebron to offer him the throne of all Israel, they said to him, "In times past, when Saul was king over us, it was you that led out and brought in Israel" (2 Samuel 5:2). We can be sure that Abner had become aware of David's military ability while David was serving under him in the armies of Saul. And Abner may have been aware of the word of the Lord to David, "You shall be shepherd of my people Israel, and you shall be prince over Israel" (2 Samuel 5:2).

Abner was sleeping beside Saul when David and Abishai entered the camp of Saul in the wilderness of Ziph. When David and Abishai had made their escape and had taken with them the king's spear and his water bottle, it was to Abner that David spoke when he called from the top of a hill with a valley between him and the army of Saul. David's words, though directed to Saul, were actually spoken to Abner. At the conclusion of this scene Abner heard Saul say to David, "Blessed be you, my son David! You will do many things and will succeed in them" (1 Samuel 26:25).

Abner was with Saul in the battle with the Philistines when Saul and Jonathan were killed on Mount Gilboa. The victory of the Philistines in this battle was so complete that the cause of Israel seemed lost forever. Abner was able to make his escape with a portion of his army. But as the conquering Philistines probably overran most of the west side of Jordan, the best that Abner could do was to set up a kingdom with Ishbosheth, the son of Saul, as king at Mahanaim, a city on the east side of Jordan. Here Abner carried on over a period of five years the effort to rehabilitate his country. He had a threefold task. He had to gradually establish the authority of Ishbosheth over the territory to the north of Judah that had been under the rule of Saul. In 2 Samuel 2:9, we read that Abner made Ishbosheth "king over Gilead and the Ashurites and Jezreel and Ephraim and Benjamin and all Israel." The language of this verse seems to indicate the steps in Abner's progress. With the collapse of the central government the various tribes probably went back to a semiautonomous government, and we have no way of knowing the extent to which Abner was able to bring them to acknowledge the rule of a throne located in a city east of Jordan.

After the battle of Gilboa, Abner remained independent. Abner was, of course, at war with the Philistines. He had never surrendered to them and doubtless avoided a direct encounter. David probably ruled at Hebron with the consent of the Philistines. But the Philistines apparently did not take full advantage of their decisive victory at Mount Gilboa, and Abner seems to have gradually wrested from them the fruits of their victory. Later, when the time comes that the leaders of the various tribes are ready to offer the throne to David, they are able to operate without the interference of the Philistines. The Philistines awake too late to the realization that Israel is united under David.

As Abner sought to re-establish the rule of the house of Saul, he inevitably found himself in conflict with David, who was ruling over Judah with Hebron as his capital. David, on his part, does not seem to have attempted to establish by conquest his authority over Israel. When he and Abishai had stood over Saul in the wilderness of Ziph, David had been unwilling to seek to gain his throne by taking Saul's life. And now that David was king of Judah he preferred to wait until the other tribes came of their own accord to offer him their allegiance and to make him king over all Israel.

It is as part of this war between the house of David and the house of Saul that we have the story of an encounter between the forces of David under Joab and the forces of Ishbosheth under Abner at Gibeon. Both commanders seem to have been aware of the danger of weakening the military might of Israel and Judah by the strife of brothers at a time when the strength of the combined kingdoms was needed for the winning of freedom from the Philistines. They attempted to settle the battle by the combat of selected men from Judah and Benjamin. This failed, and there followed a general combat in which Abner and his men were forced to flee from the forces under Joab (2 Samuel 2:12-17).

During this time of flight Abner found himself followed by Asahel, the younger brother of Joab and Abishai. Abner repeatedly warned him to turn aside and can hardly be blamed for the death of Asahel, although Joab and Abishai may have felt that the backward thrust with the butt of his spear which caught Asahel off his guard was hardly worthy of Abner. And if Abner and Asahel had fought it out in hand-to-hand combat, the outcome would not necessarily have been Abner's victory. After all, Asahel was numbered among the first thirty of David's mighty men (2 Samuel 23:24). Asahel's death at the hands of Abner created a feud between Abner and the sons of Zeruiah which was to become the cause of Abner's own death.

Perhaps the most crucial time in the life of Abner was when as the result of a quarrel with Ishbosheth he switched his allegiance from the house of Saul to the house of David. We will examine this more closely for our understanding of the character of Abner. But before doing this we will consider the tributes to him after he met his death at the hands of Joab when he and twenty men of Israel had gone to Hebron to make plans for placing David as king over all Israel.

David had no part in the death of Abner. When he first heard that Abner had died at the hands of Joab he said, "I and my kingdom are for ever guiltless before the LORD for the blood of Abner the son of Ner. May it fall upon the head of Joab, and upon all his father's house; and may the house of Joab never be without one who has a discharge, or who is leprous, or who holds a spindle, or who is slain by the sword, or who lacks bread!" (2 Samuel 3:28-29).

When David wept at the grave of Abner he lamented for him, saying,

> "Should Abner die as a fool dies?
> Your hands were not bound,
>     your feet were not fettered;
> as one falls before the wicked
>     you have fallen" (2 Samuel 3:33-34).

David continued to mourn and fast, and he said to his servants,

"Do you not know that a prince and a great man has fallen this day in Israel?"

On thinking of what the loss of Abner meant to him, David said, "I am this day weak, though anointed king; these men the sons of Zeruiah are too hard for me. The LORD requite the evildoer according to his wickedness!" (2 Samuel 3:39). But David made no effort to discipline Joab and Abishai. He had admitted that they were too hard for him.

We can be sure that David's mourning for Abner was genuine. We realize also that it was good political strategy. "All the people and all Israel understood that day that it had not been the king's will to slay Abner the son of Ner" (2 Samuel 3:37). And "When Ish-bosheth, Saul's son, heard that Abner had died at Hebron, his courage failed, and all Israel was dismayed" (2 Samuel 4:1).

Having looked at Abner's death, we return to consider the scene in which he decides to turn the kingdom over to David. The immediate occasion of the quarrel between Abner and Ish-bosheth was an affair Abner was charged with having with a concubine of Saul whose name was Rizpah. We can identify this woman with the concubine of Saul who some years later had her two sons by Saul taken along with the five sons of Merab, Saul's older daughter, to be hung in expiation for the sins of the house of Saul against the Gibeonites. It was Rizpah who through the whole of the summer guarded the bodies of these seven men of the house of Saul and protected them from the birds of the air by day and the beasts of the field by night. She guarded her dead until at the end of the summer David had the bodies of these seven, along with the bones of Saul and Jonathan, buried in the tomb of Kish in the land of Benjamin (2 Samuel 21:10-14).

Ishbosheth interpreted Abner's affair with Rizpah as the first step in an attempt by Abner to seize the throne for himself. We do not have the information necessary to know what was in Abner's mind. In the pattern of life in the ancient world, a king was very sensitive about any attempt of a man to become intimate with a concubine of the former king. When Absalom later went in to David's concubines, his followers knew that there could be no reconciliation between him and his father (2 Samuel 16:20-22; 20:3). Similarly, Solomon interpreted Adonijah's request for the hand of Abishag the Shunammite as part of his attempt to seize the throne (1 Kings 2:22). But the probability is that Abner, in his intimacy with Rizpah, which he does not deny, was guilty of fornication but not of plotting for the throne.

In any event, it was in his wrath when he was rebuked by Ishbosheth that Abner said, "God do so to Abner, and more also, if I do not accomplish for David what the LORD has sworn to him, to transfer the kingdom from the house of Saul, and set up the throne of David over Israel and over Judah, from Dan to Beersheba" (2 Samuel 3:9-10). During all the time that Abner was attempting to re-establish the house of Saul over all of Israel and Judah, he had known in his heart that he was fighting against the word of the Lord and that in the end he was certain to fail. He decided at last that instead of fighting the will of God he would become the instrument of the fulfillment of that will.

Years before, when David and Abishai had stood over the sleeping Saul, Abner was sleeping beside the king (1 Samuel 26:7). At that time David had the faith to believe that God in his own time and in his own way would establish him on the throne of Israel. It was an interesting outworking of the providence of God when Abner in his wrath with Ishbosheth decided to become the instrument of the fulfillment of God's purpose concerning David. Thus it is that God rules and overrules the passions of men, and thus his purpose was accomplished in the life of David.

# 8

## SEVEN MEN OF THE HOUSE OF SAUL—who were hanged for the sins of the house of Saul

*Scripture Background: 2 Samuel 21:1-14*

"Jesus Christ the righteous . . . is the expiation for our sins, and not for ours only but also for the sins of the whole world" (1 John 2:1-2).

"God . . . loved us and sent his Son to be the expiation for our sins" (1 John 4:10).

The story told in our passage of Scripture offends us. It violates our moral sense when we read of a man's sons and grandsons being offered up in expiation for his sins. But when we read the story we should remember that it took place nearly three thousand years ago and that it does reflect some of the basic convictions of those who lived in the age of David. And as we meditate on the story we may find that it has something to say to those who live in our contemporary world.

Our consideration of this passage will center around a number of words. The first of these is "famine." Some years after David became king, the people of Israel faced a time of famine. We are not told the cause of the famine, but we can surmise that it was due to crop failures caused by prolonged droughts. At the time of our story, the famine had lasted for three years. In an agricultural country with limited means of transportation, a series of crop failures will mean famine. The pressure of the famine undergirds this whole story. David, the king, must do something because his people are starving.

David inquires of the Lord concerning the cause of the famine. This story, like many other stories of the time of David,
assumes a situation in which men may inquire of the Lord and
hope for an answer. We do not know whether the answer came
through a prophet like Nathan or a priest like Abiathar. We do
know the answer. The Lord said: "There is blood guilt on Saul
and on his house, because he put the Gibeonites to death"
(2 Samuel 21:1).

Who were the Gibeonites? Gibeon was a city of Canaan that
was established long before the Israelites came into Palestine.
It is today the site of extensive excavations which are revealing
much about the life of ancient Canaan. When Joshua led the
Israelites in the invasion of Canaan, he and the elders of Israel
entered into a treaty of peace with the Gibeonites (Joshua,
chapter 9). It is true that the treaty of peace was achieved by
a trick on the part of the Gibeonites in which they made the
children of Israel believe that they were from a far country. But
when some of the Israelites suggested the repudiation of the
treaty, the leaders of Israel said to all the congregation: "We
have sworn to them by the LORD, the God of Israel, and now
we may not touch them" (Joshua 9:19). On the basis of this
treaty, the Gibeonites were permitted to live in the land of
Israel. They were put to hard work. They became hewers of
wood and drawers of water for all the congregation. But their
treaty rights were respected. During the whole period of the
judges, the Gibeonites lived at peace with Israel.

But when Saul became king he set out to exterminate them.
The Gibeonites describe him as "The man who consumed us and
planned to destroy us, so that we should have no place in all the
territory of Israel" (2 Samuel 21:5). The writer of Second
Samuel says that Saul sought to slay them in his zeal for Israel
and Judah. This is a zeal for Israel and Judah similar to the
zeal of Hitler for the German people when he sought to destroy
the Jews in Germany. When we remember that the lands of the
Gibeonites were in the territory of Benjamin we can guess that
part of Saul's zeal was avarice. It may be that at the time of the
drought the descendants of Saul were living on the lands of

Gibeonites who had been killed by Saul. But regardless of the reasons for it, the attempt to exterminate an innocent and peace-loving people was a dark spot in the history of Israel in the days of Saul. The Israelites as a whole may not have approved of it. But they did not oppose it. Saul as king of Israel set out to kill all of the Gibeonites. Before he completely accomplished his evil purpose, he was killed in battle with the Philistines. When David came to the throne, the persecution of the Gibeonites ceased and the remnant that was left was permitted to dwell in safety in the land. But nothing had been done to atone for the wrong that was committed. Israel had made no public act of repudiation of the policy of Saul. The story of the Gibeonites is meaningful because it is a symbol of many another act of violence in which men of power have sought to exploit and destroy those who were unable to defend themselves.

If it had not been for the famine, the Israelites probably would have forgotten all about the wrong done to the Gibeonites. But in the treaty with the Gibeonites the leaders of Israel had sworn in the presence of the God of Israel, and in the famine God was moving in judgment on Israel.

This brings us to the word "bloodguiltiness." The expression of this idea in the Bible is found first in the story of Cain and Abel. When Cain had killed his brother, the Lord said to him: "The voice of your brother's blood is crying to me from the ground" (Genesis 4:10). The God who is the vindicator of the moral order cannot permit sins of violence and exploitation to go unpunished. Israel's encounter here was not primarily with the Gibeonites. We can be sure that the remnant of the Gibeonites had hatred in their hearts for Israel in general and for the house of Saul in particular. But probably there were not enough Gibeonites left for them to be a threat to Israel. The encounter of Israel was with the God who had sent the famine in judgment on Israel because of the destruction of the Gibeonites.

The word "bloodguiltiness" is seldom used in the modern world. But the idea that lies behind this word is still with us. The people of Germany face it as they contemplate the things done by the Germans to the Jews and to others. The American people face it as they think of the suffering caused to innocent people by the dropping of the atomic bombs on Japan. They face it still more when they shrink back with horror from the thought of what they might have to do to the people of other nations if they ever use the "massive retaliation" they are so busily preparing. Individuals face it as they contemplate the wrong they have done to others and realize that God knows the things they have done and that God has ordained that men must reap what they sow.

The thought of "bloodguiltiness" leads to the word "expiation." David said to the Gibeonites: "What shall I do for you? And how shall I make expiation, that you may bless the heritage of the LORD?" (2 Samuel 21:3). David wants to know what he can do that will change the feeling of the Gibeonites toward the house of Israel. He hopes that what the Gibeonites suggest will also be acceptable to the Lord and that the Lord will remove the judgment of famine. The question of expiation is always a difficult one. Often it is impossible to make an adequate expiation. The Gibeonites rejected an expiation in terms of gold. You cannot compensate in money for thousands of men, women, and children who have been slaughtered. What expiation in gold could you make for the six million Jews who were killed by the Hitler regime in Germany? We would not approve of the expiation that the Gibeonites asked. But we can realize that it fell on the family of the man who had set out to exterminate them. We can be sure that David was not happy in granting the request of the Gibeonites. He had not sought to destroy the house of Saul. He was under oath both to Saul and to Jonathan not to seek to exterminate their descendants. He was married to Michal the daughter of Saul, and there had been a time when he had thought he would marry Merab, the older daughter of Saul (1 Samuel 18: 19). We do not know what God thought of the request of the Gibeonites. We do know that after this act of expiation had been made, God heeded the supplications for the land.

It may be better to have a somewhat distorted idea of expiation than to have no understanding of the need for it. Here again a word that has come to us from the language of sacrifice finds little use and less understanding today. But the idea is still with us. There are young Germans today who are working without pay in the heat of the territory around the Dead Sea in some effort to make expiation for the wrong done to the Jews of Germany. It was after the dropping of the bomb on Hiroshima that Dr. John Allan MacLean issued from the pulpit of the Ginter Park Presbyterian Church a call for an act of expiation on the part of the American people. This was the beginning of a movement that finally resulted in the establishment of the International Christian University of Japan. Individuals have sought in many ways to remove the bloodguiltiness resting on them.

It is against the background of the Old Testament thought of "bloodguiltiness" and the need for "expiation" that we enter into a deepened understanding of the significance of the death of Christ. If it was difficult to know what could be done to expiate the sins of the house of Saul against the Gibeonites, it is much more difficult for men to find an expiation for the sins of the world. How can sinning man be relieved of bloodguiltiness and make an expiation that will mean the restoration of the favor of God?

It is the glory of the Christian gospel that in it God makes for us the expiation we cannot make for ourselves. God loves us and has sent his Son to be the expiation for our sins. The descendants of Saul were seized by force and offered as expiation for the sin of the nation. But the Christ offered himself voluntarily as the bearer of the sins of the world. As he instituted the sacrament of the Lord's Supper, Jesus took the cup and said: "Drink of it, all of you; for this is my blood of the covenant, which is poured out for many for the forgiveness of sins" (Matthew 26:27-28). And John tells us that Jesus Christ, the righteous, "is the expiation for our sins, and not for ours only but also for the sins of the whole world" (1 John 2:2). From the picture of the seven sons of Saul offered as expiation for the sin of the nation we move to the contemplation of the great sacrifice that had to be made and has been made, the sacrifice by which the sins of the world are covered, the sacrifice which is the basis of God's offer of remission of sins to all who will put their trust in that which has been done for them in Jesus Christ.

## JOAB—captain of David's armies

*Scripture Background: 2 Samuel 10:1-14; 18:9-15; 1 Chronicles 11:6-9*

"Be of good courage, and let us play the man for our people, and for the cities of our God; and may the LORD do what seems good to him" (2 Samuel 10:12).

Joab is unquestionably one of the most interesting of the men around David. But it is very difficult to analyze his character. The intermingling of good and evil present to some extent in all of us is found to a remarkable degree in Joab. It would be easy to write him down as an evil man. But when we do this we have to realize that Joab played a part second only to David in establishing the empire of David and Solomon. If Joab had his evil deeds he also had his moments of greatness.

Joab was the brother of Abishai and Asahel. Their mother was Zeruiah, a sister of David. It would seem that Zeruiah and Abigail, the mother of Amasa, were daughters of David's mother by her first husband, a man named Nahash. Regardless of the exact nature of her relation to David, Zeruiah must have been a remarkable woman. She put iron into the lives of her sons. The sons of Zeruiah came to David in the wilderness, and David made Joab captain of the men who were with him. David and Joab together made of the six hundred men who gathered around them in the wilderness one of the greatest fighting forces of history. When we think of mighty men of battle, we are apt to think of Jackson's Stonewall Brigade or of Caesar's Tenth

Legion. But Joab and the six hundred men he commanded have a record of victory that is difficult to match. As far as we know they never lost a battle. They became the trained and disciplined core of David's armies.

There was much of evil in the life of Joab, and as we seek to understand him it is well for us to look frankly at the dark side of his life. Joab was the murderer of Abner, the commander of the armies of Saul. The story of Joab's murder of Abner must begin with the story of the death of Asahel, Joab's brother, at the hand of Abner. When David was king of Judah and Ishbosheth, the last of the sons of Saul, was ruling with the help of Abner over a portion of Israel, there was war between the house of David and the house of Saul. In one of these battles, Abner and his men were defeated by the servants of David under Joab. As Abner and his men fled, Asahel followed Abner (2 Samuel 2: 18-23). To save his own life the fleeing Abner was forced to kill Asahel with the butt of his spear. We can hardly blame Abner for this, but Joab and Abishai felt that it was necessary for them to avenge the blood of their brother. And when Abner came to David to make plans for turning the kingdom over to David, Joab treacherously murdered Abner. David accused Joab of avenging in time of peace blood that had been shed in war. But David was not man enough to discipline Joab and Abishai. He had a hard choice, because these men were invaluable to him as he sought to establish his kingdom. We do need to realize that in his murder of Abner, Joab was moving in obedience to his own code of ethics, which made him feel that he must be the avenger of blood for his brother, Asahel.

Joab went along with David in the matter of Uriah the Hittite. We can imagine that it was with a heavy heart that Joab sent Uriah to his death at the hands of the Ammonites. But Joab was loyal to David even in David's sin. While we cannot excuse Joab, we must realize that the sin of David stands out in darker terms than the sin of Joab. There is no record of Joab's ever attempting to blackmail David because of his knowledge of David's guilt.

Joab was guilty of the murder of Amasa. While we cannot defend Joab's action, we do need to see it in its setting. More

56     PERSONALITIES AROUND DAVID

than any other one man, Joab was responsible for the defeat of
Absalom; and his courageous action in putting Absalom to death
in spite of the king's command brought the rebellion to an end.
Amasa had been a traitor to David and captain of Absalom's
army. Joab was not in David's favor because he was responsible
for the death of Absalom. But it made no sense for David to
fire Joab and make Amasa captain in his place (2 Samuel 19:
11-13). And when Amasa arrived late with the reserves of
Judah after Joab and Abishai had taken decisive action in Sheba's
rebellion, Joab made short work of his cousin, Amasa, by run-
ning him through with his sword (1 Samuel 20:4-10). David
accepted Joab's action and left Joab as commander of his armies.

When Joab was an old man he followed Adonijah instead of
Solomon, who had David's support. For this he received in the
end execution by order of Solomon at the hand of Benaiah, the
son of Jehoiada. His life ended in violence. David and Solomon
were concerned for removing "bloodguiltiness" from the house
of David. But we would respect David more if he had disciplined
Joab at the time of his crimes instead of advising Solomon to do
it (1 Kings 2:1, 5-6, 28-34).

The dark side of Joab's life needs to be faced. But we must
not forget his achievements. Joab captured Jerusalem. This fortress of the Jebusites was thought to be impregnable, but Joab
led a band of men who scaled the rock on which the city was
built, took the Jebusites in the rear, and made David master of
the city (2 Samuel 5:6-7; 1 Chronicles 11:6-9). When we
think of all that Jerusalem has meant in the history of Israel,
we need to remember the part of Joab in making Jerusalem the
capital of David's empire.

We have already seen the significant part of Joab in the time
of Absalom's rebellion. Joab remained faithful to David when
it looked as if David's cause was hopeless. And in this story he
shows himself to have been in some ways a greater man than
David. He leads the forces of David in the battle. He knows
that he must disobey David in the matter of showing mercy to
Absalom. He rebukes David when David through his display of
grief is about to alienate his own men (2 Samuel 19:1-8). He

makes short work of Sheba's rebellion, and here also he seeks to avoid needless bloodshed in Israel (2 Samuel 20:14-22).

Joab's finest hour came in the midst of the war with Ammon. When the battle seemed to be going against them, the Ammonites hired an army of more than thirty thousand Syrians to come to their relief. Joab found that he and his forces were caught between two armies. The Syrians were attacking from one side and the Ammonites were attacking from the other. The situation was critical. If Joab and his army had been annihilated, the whole history of Israel might have been different. But Joab did not panic. He put part of his army under the command of Abishai and arrayed them against the Ammonites. He himself chose some of the picked men of Israel and prepared to lead a counterattack against the Syrians. And in this situation he said to his men: "Be of good courage, and let us play the man for our people, and for the cities of our God; and may the LORD do what seems good to him" (2 Samuel 10:12). Joab did not know what the outcome of the battle would be, but he called upon his followers to play the man for their people, and for the cities of their God. The outcome of the battle was in the hands of the Lord, but it was their responsibility to play the man in the time of crisis. Duties are ours. Events belong to God. Joab led Israel to a day of victory, to a victory that did much to establish the kingdom of David. But whether we face the day of victory or the time of defeat, it is our responsibility to play the man.

Joab spoke to his own soldiers, but he could also speak to us. He could speak to us as Churchill spoke to England. In a day when the odds seemed to be heavily against them, Churchill offered his people nothing but blood, sweat, and tears, and called upon them to so bear themselves that their day of battle would be Britain's finest hour. The time may come in a day of crisis in the life of America when we shall need to hear the captain of the armies of Israel saying to us: "Be of good courage, and play the man for your people, and for the cities of your God; and may the Lord do what seems good to him."

Joab spoke to men who were fighting for their very existence in the day of battle when the attack came from both the east and the west. But he can speak to us in the lesser crises of life. For many of us the real issue of life is whether we play the man when the going gets hard or seek in one way or another to avoid life's responsibilities.

There are times when life will test us. There are times when we must face the things that separate the men from the boys. Joab called upon his men to play the man for the cities of their God. The call to act as responsible men is part of God's demand on us. Jesus has said that he who puts his hand to the plow and looks back is not fit for the kingdom of God. His call to us is an imperious call, and he does not brook a halfhearted allegiance. As we fight the good fight of faith, he calls upon us to give ourselves without reserve in the service of our God.

Joab called upon his soldiers to fight like men for the people who were dependent upon them. The way in which we face life makes a lot of difference to those who stand around us. If we do our part in times of crisis, we nerve others to stand fast and to bear themselves as men.

We must face life in the readiness to say: "The Lord do what seems good to him." We cannot control what life brings us, but we can determine the way in which we deal with the things that life brings. Whether we face defeat or victory we can play the man and leave the results to God.

# 10

## ABISHAI—brother of Joab and a mighty man in battle

*Scripture Background: 1 Samuel 26; 2 Samuel 20; 21:15-17*

"The LORD forbid that I should put forth my hand against the LORD's anointed" (1 Samuel 26:11).

Abishai was son of Zeruiah and brother of Joab and Asahel. He shared with Joab the desire to avenge the death of his brother Asahel at the hands of Abner. Abner was actually killed by Joab, but Abishai was with him at the time and shared Joab's guilt for this treacherous murder of a great man. David was thinking of Abishai as well as Joab when he said: "These men the sons of Zeruiah are too hard for me. The LORD requite the evildoer according to his wickedness!" (2 Samuel 3:39).

Abishai was with Joab in the crucial battle when the army of Israel was caught between the Syrians attacking from the field and the Ammonites attacking from the city. After Joab had chosen the picked men of Israel and arrayed them against the Syrians, he put Abishai in command of the rest of the army and arrayed them against the Ammonites. Both men led their forces in counterattack, and if it is written that the Syrians fled before Joab it is also written that the Ammonites fled before Abishai (2 Samuel 10:9-14).

Abishai was with David when he fled from Jerusalem at the approach of Absalom. When Shimei cursed David it was Abishai who said to David: "Why should this dead dog curse my lord the king? Let me go over and take off his head" (2 Samuel 16:

9). Who can forget the reply of David: "Behold, my own son seeks my life; how much more now may this Benjaminite! Let him alone."

Abishai commanded one of the three divisions of David's army when the battle was joined between the forces of David and those who followed Absalom. After the death of Absalom, David placed Amasa, the captain of Absalom's defeated forces, over his armies in place of Joab. But when Amasa was slow gathering together the reserves of Judah to pursue Sheba, David placed Abishai in charge of a force made up of men from his own bodyguard to destroy Sheba before he had time to give serious trouble. Joab went with Abishai. When Amasa arrived late with the reserves, Joab ran him through with his sword and proceeded to take command of the army. Joab and Abishai brought the expedition to a successful conclusion when the men of Abel killed Sheba as the price of Joab's calling off his attack on the city (2 Samuel 20:14-22). With the conclusion of this expedition Abishai drops out of the story.

Abishai is known as the brother of Joab and second in command of the armies of Israel. In this capacity he played a most significant part in the establishment of the empire of David. He may have been in command of the armies of Israel when they conquered Edom (1 Chronicles 18:12). Probably Abishai was not the equal of Joab as a commander of men or as a military genius. But in terms of his own physical strength and his personal skill in battle he was probably superior to Joab. There emerged in the army of David a group of about thirty men who were known as David's mighty men. The story of their exploits is told in 1 Chronicles 11:10-46. Within the group of thirty men, there were three that stood out as the mightiest of David's men. Abishai did not belong to the first three, but he was second only to them and he was the commander of the thirty.

The skill of Abishai in terms of personal encounter with the enemy is revealed in a story in which he saves the life of David. In the time of David, the king was expected to actually lead his armies in battle. David continued to do this even after he had become king of all Israel. In a battle which is not specifically identified but was probably one of the two major battles in which David broke the power of the Philistines, David came very near to losing his life. There was in the army of the Philistines a giant of a man named Ishbi-benob. This man was able to handle a spear the weight of which was equal to the weight of three hundred shekels of bronze. He was armed also with a new sword. David, who was already weary, found himself engaged in battle with this giant of the Philistines. It was an unequal combat in which David might have perished. But Abishai saw the situation and came at once to David's help. This meant that Abishai had to fight and kill the giant. After this close call, David's men said to him, "You shall no more go out with us to battle, lest you quench the lamp of Israel" (2 Samuel 21:17).

The incidents which we have examined give us a picture of Abishai as a rough and ready soldier whose loyalty to David never wavered. Our particular concern now is with the story of David and Abishai in the camp of Saul. David and his men were fugitives from Saul in the wilderness of Ziph. In a move marked by boldness and daring, David and Abishai entered the camp of Saul at night. They managed to slip by the sentries and in time found themselves standing over the sleeping Saul. Abner, the captain of his army, was asleep beside the king. The king's spear and his water bottle were beside his bed. It was in this situation that David experienced an encounter with Abishai which became also his encounter with the Lord. Abishai said to David: "God has given your enemy into your hand this day; now therefore let me pin him to the earth with one stroke of the spear, and I will not strike him twice" (1 Samuel 26:8). This was Abishai's way. He believed that this was a God-given opportunity that must not be missed. When we remember Abishai's skill with weapons, we can be sure he would not have needed a second blow.

But David did not choose Abishai's way. He must, of course, have felt the attractiveness of a course of action that would put Saul out of the way and open the road to his moving toward the throne for which he had been anointed by Samuel in obedience to the word of the Lord. But David said to Abishai: "Do not destroy him; for who can put forth his hand against the LORD's anointed, and be guiltless?" (2 Samuel 26:9).

By his action in this time of crisis David revealed a profound faith in God. The faith men live by from day to day is what will guide them in a time of decision. David might have refrained from killing Saul for Jonathan's sake or for the sake of his wife Michal. But these considerations, while they may have entered his thinking, were not what determined his action. He knew that Saul was the Lord's anointed and that it was the Lord's responsibility, not his, to remove Saul. He was unwilling to do a wrong thing as a short cut to the receiving of his kingdom. It was the Lord who had sent Samuel to anoint him with oil. It was David's place to wait on the Lord. He was confident that the Lord would continue to protect him from Saul and in time would open the way for him to receive his kingdom. He did not wish to be guilty in the sight of the Lord; he preferred to remain a fugitive with a clear conscience. As he stood over Saul, David had to choose between the way of Abishai—the way of seeking a good end by an evil deed—and the way of waiting for the Lord in the confidence that the Lord could and would establish him in his throne.

The decision which David faced has its counterpart in many life situations today. The child in school may face it as he is tempted to cheat on a crucial examination in order to avoid failing the course. He needs to learn to walk the way of integrity even if he does not at the time see how he can make the grade. The businessman who is tempted to get ahead by dishonest methods should know that it is up to him to walk the way of honesty and leave his final success in the hands of the Lord. The woman who craves love and marriage may be tempted to seek to attract men by lowering her standards. She needs to know that God's plan for her will come to pass without her lowering herself to get the things she wants.

In one of the dramatic stories of history, Henry of Navarre changed his faith from Protestant to Catholic in order to open his way to the throne of France. To a casual observer it might have seemed that it was wise for him to deny his faith to gain his throne. But the consequences for him and for France and for the Protestant cause in Europe that were involved in this fatal decision can never be overestimated. If Henry had been willing to wait on the Lord he might have become king of France without walking the way of compromise. And the history of France and Europe might have been very different.

As we think of David who would not lift up his hand against the Lord's anointed to gain his throne, we think also of a greater than David to whom the tempter came and offered the kingdoms of the world and the glory of them if he would bow down and worship the evil one. Jesus repudiated at once the suggestion of entering into his kingdom through one act in which he would worship evil. The way of Abishai, the way of Joab, the way of the sons of Zeruiah, was to take what they wanted without being bothered overmuch by moral scruples. But as David in time of testing stood before the sleeping Saul, he chose not to involve himself in the guilt of Saul's destruction and to wait for the Lord to remove Saul and open the way for him to receive his kingdom. Perhaps this was one of the times in which David proved himself to be a man after God's own heart.

# 11

URIAH—the Hittite who was the husband of
Bathsheba

*Scripture Background: 2 Samuel 11*

"The ark and Israel and Judah dwell in booths; and my lord
Joab and the servants of my lord are camping in the open field;
shall I then go to my house, to eat and to drink, and to lie with my
wife? As you live, and as your soul lives, I will not do this thing"
(2 Samuel 11:11).

In the story of Uriah the Hittite, we have a picture of a man
who was himself innocent of the deep things of evil. He moves
against a background of sin and intrigue as he goes to his death
fighting in the armies of Israel. And the complete lack of suspi-
cion in the character of Uriah serves to cast in darker shadow the
infidelity of Bathsheba and the sin of David.

Uriah was a Hittite. In his racial background, he belonged to
a people who at a time some centuries before the age of David
established a great empire to the north and west of Palestine in
a land area which now is in the western part of Turkey. In the
ancient Hittite empire the Hittites established a third center of
civilization which compared not unfavorably with the civiliza-
tions of Egypt and Mesopotamia. At the time of David, groups
of Hittites were to be found in the area which is now known as
Syria. Uriah had no reason to be ashamed of the people from
whom he was descended. The modern Armenians are probably
descendants of the ancient Hittites.

Because Uriah was a Hittite he was not of the family of Israel.
His marriage to a woman of Israel and his complete acceptance

in the life of Israel are a good illustration of the process of absorption into the bloodstream of Israel of people of various racial backgrounds which was going on, particularly in Judah, during the reign of David.

Because Uriah was a Hittite he did not have in Israel a near kinsman who would be his avenger of blood if he was treacherously killed. When we read the story of Joab and Abishai and their concern to avenge the death of their brother Asahel at the hands of Abner, we know that the pattern in which a man was expected to avenge the death of a member of his own family was still present in Israel. But when the sordid facts concerning the death of Uriah became fully known there was no one in Israel to rise up as his avenger.

The Lord is the avenger of Uriah the Hittite. In the stories of David we find in David and in those around him only a limited understanding of the sense in which the Lord who has made himself known to Israel is also the God of all men. The Israelites of the age of David were so busy building the kingdom of Israel that they were not always aware of the significance of Israel for all mankind. It is interesting therefore to notice that the judgment on David which is made known at the coming of Nathan to him is the judgment of the Lord on a wrong done to Uriah, a Hittite. In Deuteronomy 10:18 we are told that the Lord "executes justice for the fatherless and the widow, and loves the sojourner." In the story of Uriah we see the Lord executing justice for the sojourner. We should notice also in this connection that the judgment which came upon Israel later in the reign of David was because of the wrong done to the Gibeonites, a people who were not of the family of Israel, by Saul and his bloody house (2 Samuel 21). Uriah was a Hittite, but he was also a devout worshiper of the God of Israel. He shows this by his reference to the Ark of the Lord as it dwells in tents, and by the complete devotion which Uriah gives to his duties as a soldier in the armies of Israel.

In Israel the real problem with the absorption of people from racial backgrounds other than that of Israel was the danger that these people who were worshipers of false gods would lead the children of Israel away from the worship of the true God. This happened, for example, when Solomon's wives turned away his heart and led him to build places of worship for false gods in Jerusalem. The basic objection to the intermarriage of the Israelites to the people of the nations around them was not racial but religious. This objection disappeared when the people of the foreign nations became genuine worshipers of the God who made himself known to Israel. Ruth, a woman of Moab, says to Naomi, "Your people shall be my people, and your God my God" (Ruth 1:16). The blessing of God was on the marriage of Ruth to Boaz, and their son, Obed, was the grandfather of David.

The probability is that Uriah's stubbornness is more than a soldier's code or loyalty to comrades in the field. It was a matter of ritual purification for the Lord's war. This is part of the concept of a holy war. Sexual intercourse was forbidden for ritual reasons. And the fidelity of Uriah to his code calls forth our admiration of him and points up the heinousness of David's sin in sending Uriah to his death.

While we may find it difficult against the background of our thought forms of today to enter into the motives of Uriah, we must realize that he acts in obedience to his understanding of the demands of the Lord on him and in a deep sense of identification with his comrades who are in the midst of the battle.

Uriah the Hittite is listed as one of David's mighty men (2 Samuel 23:39). This means that in terms of physical strength and skill in the use of the weapons of war Uriah was outstanding. We do not have to use much imagination to picture the wrath of Uriah if he had known of his wife's infidelity and of the wrong done to him by the king he served. David did not wish to provoke the wrath of Uriah.

Uriah was the husband of Bathsheba. We do not know the story of the way in which this man of the Hittites had wooed and won the hand of the woman who was one of the most beautiful of the daughters of Israel. Uriah and Bathsheba lived together in a home in Jerusalem which was near the home in which David lived. This would suggest that Uriah was a man of some substance. His home was probably in the best residential section of Jerusalem. The man who leaves a very beautiful woman for long periods of time while he is on active duty in a war is apt to have some misgivings about what may go on in his absence. But there is no indication that Uriah did not fully trust his wife.

The scene between David and Uriah is interesting. David knows that Bathsheba is with child and that if it becomes obvious that she has become pregnant while her husband is away fighting under Joab in the war with the Ammonites, Bathsheba will meet the fate of the woman guilty of adultery. In the law of Israel this was death by stoning (Leviticus 20:10; John 8:5). David has had Uriah sent to him as a messenger from Joab to report on the progress of the war. But his purpose is to have Uriah spend the night with his wife Bathsheba. In this way Bathsheba will be protected and the sin of her adultery will remain unknown.

But David in the execution of his plans runs into an unexpected stubbornness on the part of Uriah. David suggests that the conference with Uriah concerning the details of the war with the Ammonites is over and that it would now be proper for Uriah to spend the night at home with his wife. But Uriah does not go home. He sleeps at the door of the king's house with the servants of David. When David in the morning asks him why he has not gone to his home, Uriah says to David, "The ark and Israel and Judah dwell in booths; and my lord Joab and the servants of my lord are camping in the open field; shall I then go to my house, to eat and to drink, and to lie with my wife? As you live, and as your soul lives, I will not do this thing" (2 Samuel 11:11).

The position of Uriah seems stubborn and unreasonable. While we can understand his concern for his comrades who are bearing the brunt of the war with the Ammonites, we do not feel that Uriah would have harmed his comrades in any way by taking advantage of this unexpected opportunity to be for a brief time at home with his wife. But Uriah is living up to the code of the disciplined soldier. David himself gives expression to this code when, as he flees from Saul, he asks Ahimelech the priest for five loaves of bread. Ahimelech says, "I have no common bread at hand, but there is holy bread; if only the young men have kept themselves from women." David replies, "Of a truth women have been kept from us *as always when I go on an expedition*; the vessels of the young men are holy, even when it is a common journey; how much more today will their vessels be holy?" (1 Samuel 21:4-5).

Uriah does not consider himself as on leave. He has been sent as a messenger from Joab to the king, and he expects to report back to Joab as soon as his mission is accomplished. In this situation he does not feel that he can violate his code as a soldier. David is not able to make Uriah do what he feels he must not do. We may think that Uriah is stupid, but the stubborn fact of the story is that Uriah refuses to go to his home to spend the night with his wife. Uriah is a soldier. He has been enduring the hardships of a campaign. His body has been burnt with the heat of the midday sun. At night he has slept with the sky overhead. He knows the cold of the desert night and the sting of the dust storm. He knows the discomforts of war, limited rations, long marches, limited supplies of water, savage attacks by enemies. He knows that his comrades are involved in this war during the nights and days that he is in Jerusalem. He is not ready to turn aside to relax and enjoy himself until the expedition of which he is a part has accomplished its purpose. We may not wish to imitate him, but we have to admire him.

Uriah speaks to all who would seek to live in ease and comfort without bearing their part of the burden and toil of the world. It has been said that Jowett, one of the great preachers of his generation, used to always feel himself called to action by the tramp of the laboring men who went by his home early each morning. He felt that he was justified in freedom from their kind of toil only if he gave himself to the tasks laid upon him in a way that involved sacrificial living. The missionary who has stood with his comrades in the service of Christ in some difficult mission field and then has been called home often feels that he is being disloyal to the comrades with whom he has labored if he permits himself to live in luxury and ease at home.

Uriah was a soldier of the armies of Israel. He scorned a life of ease and pleasure while his comrades were bearing the brunt of the battle. When those of us who are servants of the Christ are tempted to give ourselves to the comforts and pleasures of life while our comrades in his service are enduring the hardships of the battle with evil, we need to hear Uriah the Hittite saying to us as he said to David, "As you live, and as your soul lives, I will not do this thing" (2 Samuel 11:11).

# 12

## AHITHOPHEL—David's counselor—loyalty versus expediency

*Scripture Background: 2 Samuel 15:30-37; 16:15—17:23*

"And David said, 'O Lord, I pray thee, turn the counsel of Ahithophel into foolishness' " (2 Samuel 15:31).
"The Lord had ordained to defeat the good counsel of Ahithophel, so that the Lord might bring evil upon Absalom" (2 Samuel 17:14).

David had a trusted counselor named Ahithophel. The writer of Second Samuel says of him: "Now in those days the counsel which Ahithophel gave was as if one consulted the oracle of God; so was all the counsel of Ahithophel esteemed, both by David and by Absalom" (2 Samuel 16:23). This verse is interesting because in it the writer assumes that in the world in which he lives there is such a thing as an oracle of the Lord. Samuel had been known as the seer, and people went to him even for such matters as the finding of some asses that had been lost (1 Samuel 9:5-14). And it was written of Samuel that the Lord was with him and let none of his words fall to the ground (1 Samuel 3:19). David frequently inquired of the Lord through Abiathar the priest. But Ahithophel made no claim to be a prophet of the Lord. He was a wise man, a counselor. He had a profound understanding of people and an accurate knowledge of the forces at work in the world in which he lived. People came to him for advice, and the counsel that he gave was so sound that those who knew him learned to depend on him for guidance in their major decisions. The most remarkable tribute that we have to the wisdom of the counsel of Ahithophel is the reaction of

David when he hears that Ahithophel is with Absalom. David says: "O LORD, I pray thee, turn the counsel of Ahithophel into foolishness" (2 Samuel 15:31). David knew that Absalom alone was not very dangerous, but he knew also that Absalom was to be feared if he followed the counsel of Ahithophel.

Part of the greatness of David was that he surrounded himself with wise counselors and that he was humble enough to listen to what his counselors told him and to follow their advice. David and Ahithophel had worked together in this way, and David had learned to have a profound respect for the wisdom of Ahithophel.

There was no evidence that Ahithophel was involved in the initial planning of Absalom's revolt. But as soon as Absalom had himself proclaimed king at Hebron he sent for Ahithophel from his city of Giloh (2 Samuel 15:12). When Ahithophel received this message from Absalom he had to make the major decision of his life. When a rebellion against a ruler breaks out, the first question that is asked is whether it will succeed. The people who are sympathetic to it do not wish to declare themselves unless they have reason to think that the new movement will come to power. And even those who are opposed to it do not wish to be found fighting on the losing side. Ahithophel considered Absalom's chances of success and decided that Absalom would win. He was not ignorant of the way in which over a period of years Absalom had stolen the hearts of all Israel (2 Samuel 15:1-6). He knew also that David did not have the vigor and drive of his early years. Ahithophel decided that it would be to his own advantage to cast in his lot with Absalom. We can be sure that many who had been undecided joined Absalom when they heard that Ahithophel was with him.

In making this decision Ahithophel was undoubtedly aware of factors that should have been considered. He could not have thought that Absalom would make a better king than David. He was too smart a man not to see through the front that Absalom had presented to Israel. Ahithophel knew that David had been made king because he was the Lord's anointed, and he must have known of David's reluctance to lift up his hand against the Lord's anointed even in the latter part of the reign

of Saul (1 Samuel 26:11). Ahithophel could not have believed
that it was the will of the Lord for Absalom to overthrow and
kill his father. And then there was the matter of his own loyalty
to David. David had made Ahithophel his most trusted counselor, but
he had surrounded himself with other wise advisers. One of
these was Hushai the Archite. He was known as David's friend
and was recognized as a man wise in counsel. Hushai contrasts
with Ahithophel in that while Ahithophel became a traitor to
David, Hushai decided to go out into the unknown with David
and those who were with him. He was probably an older man,
hardly able to stand the rigors of flight and life in the wilderness,
but his loyalty to David left him no alternative. David sees in the
coming of Hushai the opportunity of sending back into the city a
man who might be able to defeat the counsel of Ahithophel.

As Hushai returns to Jerusalem he reaches the city just as
Absalom and Ahithophel and those who are with them are entering the city. Absalom expresses surprise at Hushai's failure to
go with his friend. There is fine irony here as Absalom refers
to David as the friend of Hushai and not as his own father.
And Absalom, who seeks his father's life, is in no position to push
his rebuke of Hushai. He accepts Hushai's offer of allegiance at
face value and gives him a place among his counselors.

When Absalom and his party have entered the city of Jerusalem, he says to Ahithophel, "Give your counsel; what shall
we do?" (2 Samuel 16:20). Ahithophel is placed in the position
of a man who having made a wrong decision must now follow
through relentlessly as he works out the consequences of his
decision. His advice was good only in the sense that it was good
for Absalom. Ahithophel first suggests that Absalom go in to his
father's concubines in the sight of all Israel. Ahithophel knew
that this act on the part of Absalom would be recognized as a
public claim to his father's position and that it would be so
odious to David that there would be no chance of the father and
son working out a reconciliation, which would leave the support-
ers of Absalom in a difficult position. As Absalom follows the
advice of Ahithophel here, he and Ahithophel are moved by

motives that are essentially selfish. At the same time they are fulfilling the word of the Lord by the prophet Nathan to David: "Behold, I will raise up evil against you out of your own house; and I will take your wives before your eyes, and give them to your neighbor, and he shall lie with your wives in the sight of this sun. For you did it secretly; but I will do this thing before all Israel, and before the sun" (2 Samuel 12:11-12).

When he knows that the break between Absalom and David is irrevocable, Ahithophel offers to lead at once an expeditionary force of twelve thousand men with the express purpose of capturing and killing David before he has had time to make good his escape.

Ahithophel's conscience must have twinged a little at the thought of being the one to find and kill the man to whom he had been for many years a trusted counselor. But Ahithophel has penetrated to the heart of the struggle. He and Joab are agreed on at least one thing. They both know that the choice is between Absalom and David. If David is slain in battle, the men who follow him will have nothing to fight for. Those who were with David told him the same thing a little later when David wanted to go out with them to the battle between his army and the army of Absalom. We do not know whether or not Ahithophel would have been able to succeed in his quick dash to seize the king and end the struggle, but certainly David was afraid of the counsel of Ahithophel.

When Hushai seeks to defeat the counsel of Ahithophel his purpose is clear. He wants to give David time to make good his escape and to gather together an army with which he can defeat the forces commanded by Absalom. Hushai begins by playing upon the fears of those who follow Absalom. He makes a valid point when he warns of the dangers of a sudden attack on David and those who are with him. David is indeed expert in war. He has with him the core of his professional army, including such experienced commanders as Joab and Abishai and Ittai the Gittite. So far as we know, Joab had never lost a battle. Would he have lost this one? The exploits of David's mighty men were well known. The knowledge of the skill in battle of the men they had to fight could bring terror to the hearts of those who were with Absalom.

Having aroused the fears of the people, Hushai plays on the vanity of Absalom as he pictures him at the head of an army so powerful that the forces under David would be completely overwhelmed. His closing pictures of the success of Absalom border on the ridiculous, but by this time he has caught the enthusiasm and imagination of the crowd. Absalom and those who are with him say, "The counsel of Hushai the Archite is better than the counsel of Ahithophel" (2 Samuel 17:14). The writer of the story sees in this decision the hand of the Lord as he is moving to bring judgment to Absalom.

When his advice is rejected, Ahithophel walks away from the council table and saddles his ass and rides alone to his own city of Giloh. He takes time to set his house in order and then he hangs himself (2 Samuel 17:23). We cannot fully enter into the motives that led to his act of self-destruction, but it is hard to overestimate his chagrin when his counsel was rejected. And Ahithophel was wise enough to know that when the counsel of Hushai was adopted, the cause of Absalom was lost. He did not have the courage to face the returning David.

Why did Ahithophel, who was one of the wisest men of his time, make such a mess of his own life? What was the fatal flaw in the character of Ahithophel? The answer is that Ahithophel failed because he did not know the meaning of an absolute loyalty. In the great decision of his life he did what he thought was the expedient thing rather than what he knew was the right thing. Ahithophel should have gone into exile with David even if it looked at the time as if Absalom was sure to win. If he had remained faithful to David, Ahithophel would have been known as both wise and good. As it is, he is remembered as a traitor and a suicide.

# 13

## ABIATHAR—the priest who gave the word of the Lord

*Scripture Background: 1 Samuel 21:1—23:18; 30:7-10; 2 Samuel 2:1; 15:24-29; 19:11-15; 20:25; 1 Kings 1; 2:26-27; 1 Chronicles 18:16; 24:3, 6, 31*

"And David said to Abiathar the priest, the son of Ahimelech, 'Bring me the ephod.' So Abiathar brought the ephod to David. And David inquired of the LORD" (1 Samuel 30:7-8).

Abiathar was a priest who was closely associated with David. He came to David in the wilderness as the result of Saul's stupid and brutal slaughter of the priests of Nob. Ahimelech, the father of Abiathar, was priest at Nob during most of the time of Saul. David fled to Nob immediately after the great scene in which he and Jonathan renewed their covenant of friendship. He arrived at Nob alone, without weapons of any kind, and hungry. David did not tell the truth to Ahimelech when the priest questioned him concerning the purpose of his coming. He professed to be on an urgent mission for the king and asked for food for himself and for the men he said he expected to meet him. Ahimelech gave him the shewbread that had just been removed from the altar. In response to his request for a weapon Ahimelech gave him the sword of Goliath of Gath, which had been kept in the sanctuary as a trophy. Doeg the Edomite, Saul's chief herdsman, was in Nob that day and heard the conversation between David and Ahimelech. David went from Nob to Achish, the king of the Philistines, but as he felt that his life was in danger there, he feigned madness to make his escape and went to the cave of Adullam near to Bethlehem. There he began to gather around him the members of his own family and others until he became the leader of a band of soldiers numbering from four to six hundred men.

The story of David's visit to the high priest at Nob is referred to in the New Testament (Mark 2:26). There is a confusion of names here as the reference is to Abiathar rather than Ahimelech, and this confusion is found also in some of the references in Chronicles (1 Chronicles 18:16; 24:3, 6, 31). We will assume here that Ahimelech was high priest at Nob under Saul and that Abiathar followed him as high priest, along with Zadok, under David. The story is referred to in the New Testament as an illustration from the Old Testament of the priority of human need over ritual observances. Jesus used it to defend his disciples when they ate some of the grain as they were passing through a field of wheat on the Sabbath day. In both cases, the ministering to human hunger was understood to be more important than obedience to the details of the law.

When Saul asks the men of Benjamin for help against the son of Jesse, Doeg the Edomite reports that he has seen Ahimelech give food and weapons to David. He must have known that his report was distorted, because if he heard the conversation between David and Ahimelech he knew that Ahimelech was unaware that David was in flight from Saul. When Ahimelech was summoned by Saul, he protested his innocence of wrongdoing against the king and referred to David as the king's son-in-law. But Saul ordered the death of Ahimelech and all the priests of Nob. This was an order that Saul's soldiers refused to obey. They were prepared to risk the wrath of Saul rather than to lift their hands against the priests of the Lord. Doeg the Edomite had no such scruples, and when Saul gave him permission to attack the priests, Doeg and his ruffians were only too glad to respond. In the raid on Nob that followed, eighty-five priests were put to death. Their wives and children were also slain. The Israelites never had any respect for the Edomites, and Doeg the Edomite lived up to the pattern of many of his people as a man without either conscience or religion. Of all the acts of

Saul, the slaughter of the priests was perhaps the most inexcusable, both in terms of its moral enormity and because of its sheer stupidity. When Abiathar made his escape and fled to David, carrying an ephod in his hand, it meant that the blessing of the prophets was on David and that the man who by birth was in line to become the high priest was with him.

By the time Abiathar escaped, David had left the stronghold of Adullam, and on the advice of Gad the prophet, was hiding in the wilderness in the southern part of Judah. When Abiathar came to David and told his story, David said to him, "I knew on that day, when Doeg the Edomite was there, that he would surely tell Saul. I have occasioned the death of all the persons of your father's house. Stay with me, fear not; for he that seeks my life seeks your life; with me you shall be in safekeeping" (1 Samuel 22:22-23).

Abiathar was a great help to David. David turned to him as the priest with the ephod of the high priest to inquire of him the will of the Lord. This ephod was an upper garment worn by the high priest when he was about his official duties. With it were the Urim and Thummim (Exodus 28:30). By using the Urim and Thummim, the high priest learned the will of God in doubtful cases. These may have been stones carried in a pocket attached to the breastplate of the high priest to betoken his authority to obtain light and truth that he might seek the counsel of the Lord. We do not know how the will of the Lord was made known to the high priest; the stones may have been used in the casting of a lot. Another suggestion which we find in the Westminster Bible Dictionary is: "He [the high priest] laid the matter humbly before God in prayer; the answer dawned in his mind; he believed that the response was correct, because he had made his request in the manner of God's appointment, and because he had God's promise that he should receive light and truth. The answer was inward illumination, without any external sign, and finds its parallel in the revelations granted to the prophets."

Although we do not know just how the message was communicated, we know that David consistently sought to learn through

Abiathar the will of the Lord and that he received answers which were the guide to his conduct. Shortly after Abiathar came to him, David heard that the Philistines were attacking Keilah, a city in the south of Judah. David inquired of the Lord whether he should go to the relief of Keilah. The answer was, "Go and attack the Philistines and save Keilah" (1 Samuel 23:2). David's men were not enthusiastic about the undertaking. We can understand their point of view when they said, "Behold, we are afraid here in Judah; how much more then if we go to Keilah against the armies of the Philistines?" (1 Samuel 23:3). David inquired of the Lord again and received the answer, "Arise, go down to Keilah; for I will give the Philistines into your hand" (1 Samuel 23:4). This battle against the Philistines in obedience to the word of the Lord received through Abiathar was the first battle of David and his men after David's flight from the court of Saul. It was a daring thing for this little band of fugitives to seek to bring relief to besieged Keilah. The battle ended in victory, the first victory of what became a disciplined fighting force that was never defeated.

After David's victory over the Philistines at Keilah, Saul hears that David and his men are there and plans to catch them within the walled city. When word of this comes to David, he says to Abiathar, "Bring the ephod here." He then puts his question, "O Lord, the God of Israel, thy servant has surely heard that Saul seeks to come to Keilah, to destroy the city on my account. Will the men of Keilah surrender me into his hand? Will Saul come down, as thy servant has heard? O Lord, the God of Israel, I beseech thee, tell thy servant." The answer is, "He will come down." To the question, "Will the men of Keilah surrender me and my men into the hand of Saul?" the answer is, "They will surrender you" (1 Samuel 23:6-14). After receiving this answer, David leaves Keilah.

In a similar manner, David inquires of the Lord as to whether or not he shall pursue after the Amalekites who have sacked Ziklag and carried away the wives, the children, and the possessions of David and his men. He receives the answer, "Pursue; for you shall surely overtake and shall surely rescue" (1 Samuel

30:8). David acts upon this word of the Lord. Their wives and children are saved, and their possessions are recovered. After his return, when he has heard of the death of Saul and has observed a period of mourning, David inquires of the Lord, "Shall I go up into any of the cities of Judah?" The answer comes, "Go up." To the question, "To which shall I go up?" the answer is, "To Hebron" (2 Samuel 2:1).

When David has been made king of all Israel and the full force of the Philistines has been gathered against him, David once more inquires of the Lord, "Shall I go up against the Philistines? Wilt thou give them into my hand?" The Lord says to David, "Go up; for I will certainly give the Philistines into your hand" (2 Samuel 5:19). Before the second of the two decisive battles that forever broke the power of the Philistines, David inquires of the Lord and receives the answer: "You shall not go up; go around to their rear, and come upon them opposite the balsam trees. And when you hear the sound of marching in the tops of the balsam trees, then bestir yourself; for then the LORD has gone out before you to smite the army of the Philistines" (2 Samuel 5:17-25).

We have listed these various incidents in which David sought the will of the Lord to point out the obvious fact that David through Abiathar was able to inquire of the Lord and receive answers which should become the guides to his conduct. David was dealing here with the living God who made his will known in times of decision in David's life. Men cannot manipulate this. There are times when the Lord does not answer. When Saul saw the army of the Philistines before the battle of Gilboa, he was afraid. He inquired of the Lord, but the Lord did not answer him, "either by dreams, or by Urim, or by prophets" (1 Samuel 28:6). It was at this time that Saul ceased to inquire of the Lord and turned to witchcraft and the powers of evil.

After David was established on the throne of all Israel, Abiathar became high priest along with Zadok. He and Zadok remained faithful to David at the time of Absalom's rebellion. As David fled toward the wilderness to escape from Absalom, Abiathar and Zadok, and all the Levites with them, came to him, bringing the Ark of the Lord, and set down the Ark until all

David's followers had passed out of the city. Then David told them to take the Ark back to Jerusalem. He knew that the presence of the Lord was not determined by the possession of the Ark. Their sons, Ahimaaz and Jonathan, became the messengers to David of the success of Hushai in defeating the counsel of Ahithophel.

For some reason, unknown to us, Abiathar as an old man joined with Joab in supporting Adonijah's bid for the throne. When Adonijah's second attempt failed and his execution was ordered, Joab also was put to death by order of Solomon. Solomon spared the life of Abiathar in recognition of his great services to David his father, but he put him out of his position as high priest and banished him to his estate at Anathoth, the city of the priests. This order against Abiathar meant also that the line of succession of high priests passed from the house of Eli and that the word of the Lord spoken to Samuel concerning the house of Eli was fulfilled (1 Samuel 3:14).

In spite of the cloud that falls on him at the end of his life, Abiathar stands out as one of the great men of the age of David.

The story of Abiathar is of special significance because in these documents which are about three thousand years old we have the picture of a priest who in some way we cannot fully understand was the medium through whom the Lord made known his will to David. Many Old Testament scholars have tried to explain away such experiences, but we do violence to the entire Old Testament narrative when we treat it in this fashion.

We do not know a great deal about the character of Abiathar. We do know that he takes his place in that long line of persons through whom the word of the Lord has come to man. We believe that God has spoken unto the fathers in many and various ways through prophets and priests. We give thanks that he has also spoken unto us through his Son.

# 14

## NATHAN—the prophet whom the Lord sent to David

*Scripture Background: 2 Samuel 7; 12:1-15, 24-25; 1 Kings 1;*
*1 Chronicles 22:6-16; 29:29; 2 Chronicles 9:29*

"The thing that David had done displeased the LORD. And the LORD sent Nathan to David" (2 Samuel 11:27 and 12:1).

Nathan the prophet is one of the most significant of the figures of the age of David. David was anointed by Samuel at the command of the Lord. In one of his flights from Saul, David came to Samuel at Ramah (1 Samuel 19:18-24). But Samuel died while David was still a fugitive. Nathan was active as a prophet during the whole of the reign of David and part of the reign of Solomon. Another prophet named Gad appeared when David was fleeing from Saul, to advise David to leave the stronghold of Adullam and go into Judah (1 Samuel 22:5). He appeared again with the word of the Lord to David concerning the census (2 Samuel 24). Ahijah was active as a prophet in the reign of Solomon. But when we think of the prophet during the time of David we think always of Nathan.

The word of the Lord that comes through the prophets represents an essential part of the picture in any study of the age of David. As the word of the Lord comes through the prophets we see God moving in the context of history in both judgment and mercy. It is possible that we owe much of our knowledge of the history of Israel in the time of David to the writing of Nathan (1 Chronicles 29:29; 2 Chronicles 9:29).

Nathan is the bearer of the word of the Lord which comes

to David in connection with his desire to build the temple of the Lord. We would judge that it was through Nathan that David received the word of the Lord to which he referred when he said to Solomon: "My son, I had it in my heart to build a house to the name of the LORD my God. But the word of the LORD came to me, saying, 'You have shed much blood and have waged great wars; you shall not build a house to my name, because you have shed so much blood before me upon the earth. Behold, a son shall be born to you; he shall be a man of peace. I will give him peace from all his enemies round about; for his name shall be Solomon, and I will give peace and quiet to Israel in his days. He shall build a house for my name' " (1 Chronicles 22:7-10). David did not give the name of the prophet who was the bearer of this word of the Lord to him, but the probability is that the prophet was Nathan.

Nathan is the bearer of the significant prophecy concerning the permanence of the house of David which we find in 2 Samuel 7:4-17. This prophecy profoundly influenced the Messianic expectation in Israel. It was fulfilled in part when the house of David remained on the throne of Judah during the whole of the history of the Southern Kingdom. It was fulfilled in a deeper dimension when the angel Gabriel said to Mary concerning her son, Jesus:

> ". . . the Lord God will give to him the throne of his father David,
> and he will reign over the house of Jacob for ever;
> and of his kingdom there will be no end" (Luke 1:32-33).

At the time of Solomon's birth it was Nathan who brought a special message from the Lord and who called the child by a name that meant "beloved of the Lord" (2 Samuel 12:24-25). Some interpreters have concluded that Nathan was probably the tutor of Solomon. Unquestionably he played a very significant part in bringing to defeat the bid of Adonijah for the throne and in establishing Solomon securely on the throne of Israel (1 Kings 1:5-48).

The crucial scene in the life of Nathan is when the Lord

sends him to David after David has brought about the death of Uriah the Hittite and has taken Bathsheba, the wife of Uriah, to be his wife. David has been a devout worshiper of the Lord, but in this story he is seen as a man who has been led by one wrong step to move ever more deeply in the way of evil. He had become guilty of adultery with Bathsheba while Uriah was with Joab in the expedition against the Ammonites. This led to Bathsheba's pregnancy. The pregnancy if discovered and not explained could lead to Bathsheba's being stoned to death. In an effort to cover his sin, David had Uriah brought home, but Uriah's stubborn refusal to spend the night with his wife meant the failure of this effort. David then felt forced to write a note to Joab with the suggestion that Uriah be put in the most dangerous place in the battle. When Uriah died in a battle with the Ammonites and Bathsheba's period of mourning was over, David immediately took her as his wife. As the months passed, he tried to act as if nothing had happened. Then Bathsheba gave birth to a son. There may have been some talk around the palace, but David probably thought the whole matter was ended.

However, the thing which David had done displeased the Lord. Nathan does not come to David of his own accord. He comes because the Lord has sent him, and David in his sin is confronted with the word of the Lord. Nathan evidently had information concerning the sin of David which had come to him from the Lord. In a similar manner, Elijah knew of the sin of Ahab when he confronted the guilty king in Naboth's vineyard (1 Kings 21) and Elisha knew of the sin of Gehazi when the servant returned from following after Naaman (2 Kings 5). It is impossible to ignore this knowledge of the Hebrew prophets.

Nathan does not begin by a direct accusation of David. Instead he tells a carefully framed story of the wrong which a rich man has done to a poor man. And it is only after he has received David's judgment, "The man who has done this deserves to die" (2 Samuel 12:5), that Nathan says to David, "You are the man."

The offense of David's sin is seen against the background of all that the Lord had done for David. The Lord had taken him from the sheepfold and had delivered him out of the hand of

Saul and had made him king over all Israel. The Lord had promised to establish his house as the ruling dynasty. David's sin was aggravated by the fact that he had been lifted high in the presence of Israel as a man after God's own heart. By his sin David had given great occasion to the enemies of the Lord to blaspheme.

The heart of the sin of David is expressed in the indictment, "Why have you *despised the word of the Lord, to do what is evil in his sight?* You have smitten Uriah the Hittite with the sword, and have taken his wife to be your wife, and have slain him with the sword of the Ammonites" (2 Samuel 12:9). Nathan tears away any pretense which David may have built up about Uriah's having met death in the battle with the Ammonites. He places the responsibility for Uriah's death where it belongs. David is as guilty as if he had slain Uriah with his own hands. A little later Nathan sums up his indictment as he says to David, *"By this deed you have utterly scorned the Lord"* (2 Samuel 12:14). David's sin has involved the wrong to Uriah and the wrong to Bathsheba and the wrong to the child born under the shadow of adultery. But the deepest dimension of David's sin is that he has despised the word of the Lord and utterly scorned the Lord. Adultery and murder are not merely sins against people; they are arrogant violations of the law of the Lord.

Nathan brings to David the judgment of the Lord. The Lord who is the vindicator of the moral order cannot permit the sin of David to go unrecognized and unpunished. We are dealing here with what is usually called retribution—the pattern of life in which the Lord so orders the affairs of men that they do not avoid reaping the consequences of their evil deeds. Men think that they can mock God and violate his laws with impunity. But God is not mocked. Men reap what they sow. Nathan tells David that because he has slain Uriah with the sword of the Ammonites the sword will never depart from his house. He continues: "Thus says the LORD, 'Behold, I will raise up evil against you out of your own house; and I will take your wives before your eyes, and give them to your neighbor, and he shall lie with your wives in the sight of this sun. For you did it secretly;

but I will do this thing before all Israel, and before the sun' "
(2 Samuel 12:11-12).

The consequences of wrongdoing frequently come to a man
in ways related to the sins he has committed. David has taken
the sword, and the sword will not depart from his house. We do
not have to look far into the future to see Absalom slaying
Amnon and seeking the life of his father. David has sinned in
terms of adultery, and similar sins will plague his home. We
think at once of Amnon and Tamar and of Absalom's going
in to his father's wives. David's sin has been in secret, but retribution when it comes is in the open. The sin of David becomes
known, and the sins of his children are before all Israel.

When David is faced with the word of judgment through
Nathan the prophet, he says to Nathan, "I have sinned against
the LORD." And Nathan says to David, "The LORD also has put
away your sin; you shall not die." In these simple statements
are condensed two tremendous experiences. The first is the
experience of repentance. The second is forgiveness offered and
received. The brevity of David's statement must not lead us to
underestimate the searching nature of his repentance. In repentance a man owns his sin, accepts full responsibility for it, and
acknowledges his guilt before God. In repentance a man disowns
his sin and puts it from him as no longer representative of the
person he now is. The Fifty-first Psalm is attributed to David.
Whether David wrote it or not, it is a genuine expression of the
experience of repentance. It is a description of an experience of
repentance through which David must have passed.

Nathan tells David that the Lord has put away his sin. This
means that the Lord has accepted David's repentance and has
put away his sin so that it can no longer come between him and
his God. David does not know of the great sacrifice by which the
Lord will cover sin and open the way for the offer of forgiveness
to all who will receive it. He does know that there is forgiveness
with the Lord. God has restored the broken relation and accepted
David again as his servant. Here is the word of grace that goes
along with the word of judgment.

But the word of forgiveness does not remove all the consequences of sin. It is after David has received the word of forgiveness that the final word is spoken. Nathan says, "Because by this deed you have utterly scorned the LORD, the child that is born to you shall die" (2 Samuel 12:14). Here and throughout his life David met the judgments of the Lord not as one who was old and hardened in sin but as one who had been forgiven and was facing the discipline of the Lord as a child of God. Through the judgments of the Lord it was made clear to all Israel that the thing that David had done had displeased the Lord. The Lord does not deal lightly with adultery and murder, and David's forgiveness did not mean that men can sin with impunity. It did mean that David, forgiven and restored, could continue to be the anointed of the Lord, the servant of the Lord in his generation.

# 15

## THREE MIGHTY MEN—who risked their lives for David

*Scripture Background: 2 Samuel 23:13-17; 1 Chronicles 11:15-19; 2 Samuel 18:3; 21:15-17; 1 Chronicles 12:16-18; 1 Samuel 7: 6*

"He poured it out to the LORD" (2 Samuel 23:16).

The story of the exploit of three of David's mighty men in breaking through the army of the Philistines and drawing water from the well of Bethlehem is well known as one of the great stories of daring and devotion. Before seeking to understand the meaning of the story, we need to look at its setting. As it is told in 2 Samuel 23:13-17 and repeated in 1 Chronicles 11:15-19, the place of the story in the life of David is not identified. And the significance of the story is in part independent of our ability to fit it accurately into the story of the life of David as a whole.

Kirkpatrick in the Cambridge Bible on Second Samuel places the story at the time of the invasion of the Philistines described in 2 Samuel 5:17-21. There are good reasons for this identification. Both stories take place in the valley of Rephaim, which Kirkpatrick describes as "an open plain or upland valley, stretching in a southwest direction from the neighbourhood of Jerusalem towards Bethlehem." The setting of the story is at a time when David was at war with the Philistines rather than during the time that he was a fugitive from Saul. According to this identification the exploit of three of David's mighty men comes after David has been made king over all Israel and after David and Joab have captured Jerusalem and made this fortress the center of their operations. This would fit into the story as a whole, for at this time in David's life it was becoming evident to all that he was the leader raised up of God for the deliverance of Israel from the Philistines.

When the Philistines awoke to the fact that all Israel was united under David and that David had captured Jerusalem, they realized that it was necessary for them to make at once an all-out effort to crush him before he had time to bring into the struggle the full strength of Israel. They gathered together all of their forces and invaded Judah by the way of the valley of Rephaim. David did not wait for the Philistines to attack; he marched to meet them. In the battle that followed and in a second battle that was fought in the same general area, David broke the power of the Philistines and ended their threat to the life of Israel. The drawing of the water from the well of Bethlehem probably took place while David was waiting for the opportune time to launch his attack on the Philistines.

While David was in the stronghold and the army of the Philistines was in the valley, with a garrison in Bethlehem, three of his mighty men heard him say, "O that some one would give me water to drink from the well of Bethlehem which is by the gate!" (2 Samuel 23:15). David was remembering the peaceful days of his boyhood when he had quenched his thirst with water from the well of Bethlehem. We can all understand the yearning of a man in the heat of summer for the cool water he had enjoyed as a boy.

Without David's knowing it the three mighty men slipped away, determined to get for him some water from the well of Bethlehem. We do not know who these three men were. They were not the first three that stood out as the mightiest of David's mighty men. A very likely suggestion is that Abishai, the chief of the thirty, was one of the three and that Benaiah, the son of Jehoiada, was with them. We cannot prove this. We do know that these three men broke through the garrison of the Philistines, drew water from the well of Bethlehem, and made their way back through Philistine-infested territory and presented the water to David.

There is a sense in which the deed of these men was the height of folly. Men have no right to risk their lives simply to satisfy a whim of their commander. David could have gotten all the water he needed from other sources of supply. If these men had perished in their undertaking it would properly have been pronounced a deed of folly. But we cannot help being moved at this expression of the devotion of David's men. In commenting on it, Kirkpatrick describes it as "A striking proof of the enthusiam which David inspired in his followers, and a noble instance of the true spirit of chivalry, which fears no danger and shrinks from no self-sacrifice, in order to do the smallest service for the object of its devotion; the spirit which is perfected in the highest example of love (John 15:13)."

The devotion of David's mighty men was in part a personal reaction to David as a leader of men. It was based also on the recognition of David as anointed of the Lord, as a man raised up by God for the salvation of his people. This idea is brought out by the tribute of the men of Benjamin and Judah who came to David when he was a fugitive from Saul. David went out to meet them and said, "If you have come to me in friendship to help me, my heart will be knit to you; but if to betray me to my adversaries, although there is no wrong in my hands, then may the God of our fathers see and rebuke you." Then the Spirit came upon Amasai, chief of the thirty, and he said,

> "We are yours, O David;
>     and with you, O son of Jesse!
> Peace, peace to you,
>     and peace to your helpers!
> For your God helps you" (1 Chronicles 12:16-18).

A similar recognition of the significance of David was expressed by his men when he was rescued by Abishai from an unequal struggle with the giant Ishbi-benob. They said to him, "You shall no more go out with us to battle, lest you quench the lamp of Israel" (2 Samuel 21:17). And when David offered to join his men in the battle against Absalom they said, "You shall not go out. For if we flee, they will not care about us. If half of us die, they will not care about us. But you are worth ten thousand of us" (2 Samuel 18:3).

A remarkable expression of devotion came from Ittai the Gittite when he and his men joined David as he was fleeing from Absalom. David said to Ittai, "Why do you also go with us? Go back, and stay with the king; for you are a foreigner, and also an exile from your home. You came only yesterday, and shall I today make you wander about with us, seeing I go I know not where? Go back, and take your brethren with you; and may the LORD show steadfast love and faithfulness to you." But Ittai answered the king, "As the LORD lives, and as my lord the king lives, wherever my lord the king shall be, whether for death or for life, there also will your servant be" (2 Samuel 15:19-21).

The devotion of David's men is symbolized by the bottle of water from the well of Bethlehem which was handed to him by three of his mighty men while he was in the stronghold of Adullam. But David did not drink the water. He considered it too precious to drink. Instead of drinking it, he poured it out as an offering to the Lord. The pouring out of water was one form of making an offering to the Lord. When Samuel gathered the Israelites together at Mizpah, we read that they "drew water and poured it out before the LORD, and fasted on that day, and said there, 'We have sinned against the LORD' " (1 Samuel 7:6). Concerning this act on the part of David, Dean Stanley comments: "That which had been won by the lives of those three gallant chiefs was too sacred for him to drink, but it was on that very account deemed by him as worthy to be consecrated in sacrifice to God, as any of the prescribed offerings of the Levitical ritual. Pure Chivalry and pure Religion there formed an absolute union."

When David poured out as an offering to the Lord the water brought to him by his three mighty men at the risk of their lives, he offered to the Lord the devotion of his men. When men recognize in a leader a person who has been anointed of the

Lord and raised up of God as the peculiar instrument of his purpose, they are apt to give to him as leader a high degree of loyalty and devotion. And the man who has received in this way the complete loyalty of those who are his followers is apt to be put in a place of great temptation. His temptation is to use the devotion of those who follow him for his personal aggrandizement rather than to dedicate the loyalty of his men to the service of God.

In times of chaos and confusion people are looking desperately for a leader they can trust. And when a leader emerges whom they feel is sent of God for their deliverance they rally around him with a devotion that often has about it a mystic element. We need only to think of the loyalty given to Hitler as "the Leader" when he first appeared on the scene in Germany and of the way in which that loyalty was betrayed. A more recent example is the loyalty of the Cuban people to Castro as the leader of the revolution in Cuba and of the way in which they were betrayed into a dictatorship more terrible than that from which they had sought to escape.

We find this sort of thing in the life of a church. A congregation in calling a pastor seeks to have a man come to them whom they believe to have been sent of God to lead them into his purpose for them. In such a situation they may give to their minister a loyalty that is part of their service of God. This is satisfactory if the minister consistently dedicates to the service of God in that community the loyalty he receives. But if the minister uses the loyalty and devotion of his people for his own selfish purposes he has betrayed the trust he received as a man sent of God.

On the political scene, we live in a world in which many nations are trying to move from the chaos and confusion of life in the past into the building of a society in which there is equality of opportunity for all. The peoples of the world are seeking leaders who can be trusted. But the leader who can be trusted is the leader who has a high sense of responsibility to God, the leader who is willing to dedicate to the tasks that God has set for him the love and devotion which he receives from those who follow him.

Even Jesus came as the anointed of the Lord. He came not to do his own will but to do the will of the Father who had sent him. He calls to men to follow him and to give to him a devotion that is absolute. He has a right to ask this devotion because he sets his followers to the tasks of God in their generation. The service of the Christ is the service of the God who sent him.

# 16

MICHAL—the daughter of Saul who was childless

*Scripture Background: 1 Samuel 18:17-29; 19:8-17; 25:44; 2 Samuel 3:12-16; 6:12-23; 1 Chronicles 15:25-29*

"And Michal the daughter of Saul had no child to the day of her death" (2 Samuel 6:23).

Michal, the younger daughter of Saul, was the first woman in David's life. The story of her marriage to David is interwoven with the intrigue of the court of Saul. As his jealousy of David grows, Saul hopes that David will perish at the hand of the Philistines. He says to David: "Here is my elder daughter Merab; I will give her to you for a wife; only be valiant for me and fight the LORD's battles" (1 Samuel 18:17). When David is not killed in battle, Saul goes back on his promise and gives his daughter Merab to Adriel the Meholathite.

Michal, Saul's younger daughter, loves David. We can understand this. David was brave in battle. He was gifted in music and in dancing. He was the bosom friend of her brother, Jonathan. Saul does not think of Michal's happiness. His only thought is that Michal may be a snare for David. Through his servants he passes the word on to David that it is still possible for him to become the king's son-in-law. But he also names the price at which he will be willing to give his daughter Michal to David in marriage. As the proof of the death of his enemies, he asks for a hundred foreskins of the Philistines. David accepts the challenge. He leads his men into a battle in which two hundred

Philistines are killed. He delivers the tokens of his victory to Saul, and the marriage of David and Michal, the daughter of Saul, is consummated. As we look at these events through the eyes of Michal, we are bound to wonder concerning her feelings as she sees her father using her as bait for a snare in his effort to destroy David. Saul does not grow in our estimation as we think of his part in this story. Later, David refers to this incident when he asks Ishbosheth to send Michal back to him (2 Samuel 3:14).

Michal soon found that as daughter of Saul and wife of David, she was torn between loyalty to her father and love for her husband. She lived in the same inner conflict that marked the life of her brother Jonathan. Michal gave her first loyalty to her husband. This was revealed on the night she saw soldiers surrounding their home. She warned David and arranged for him under the cover of night to leave the house through a window. She then put an image in the bed and placed a pillow of goats' hair at its head. (We cannot help wondering what David and Michal were doing with an image in the house.) In the morning, Michal fooled the soldiers by pointing to the figure in the bed and telling them that David was sick. The soldiers reported to Saul and later returned in obedience to his command, "Bring him up to me in the bed, that I may kill him" (1 Samuel 19:15). But before they returned, David had the time needed to make his escape. When Saul accused Michal of having tricked him, she lied to her father, saying: "He said to me, 'Let me go; why should I kill you?'" As we think on this story we are bound to raise some questions about the ethics of Michal's behavior. But we must ask: Do men have a right to truth from a woman when they are seeking the life of her husband?

David fled to begin a life in which for several years he was hiding from Saul. Saul gave Michal in marriage to a man named Paltiel, the son of Laish. We do not know just how long Michal lived with Paltiel. But as she was married to him before the death of Saul, it must have been for a period of at least seven or eight years. When David's years of hiding were ended, he became king of Judah and reigned at Hebron for seven years. And it was toward the end of this period that the negotiations between him and Abner took place. When Abner asked for a conference with David, David's first condition was the return of Michal, his wife. In making this demand, David was probably moved by mixed motives. He undoubtedly wanted to claim Michal as his wife. And we can be reasonably certain that he hoped that a son born to him and Michal would unite the house of David and the house of Saul and become the means of bringing peace to Israel.

We do not know just how happy Michal and Paltiel had been together. We do know that as Abner and his soldiers escorted Michal toward the border of David's kingdom, her husband Paltiel followed after her weeping. It would be interesting to speculate on the inner thoughts of this woman as, again a pawn in politics, she is being taken from Paltiel and returned to David. We can sympathize with Abner as he puts up with Paltiel's weeping until they come to the border that marks the end of the kingdom of Ishbosheth and the beginning of the kingdom of David. It is then that he says to Paltiel: "Go, return." And Paltiel returns. Michal goes on to find herself again the wife of David, king of Judah. She finds also that in the meantime David has added other wives, and that he has children by them. Michal is with David as the wife of his youth when he is made king over all Israel. She moves with him from Hebron to Jerusalem and takes her place in the home that is established in Jerusalem.

A significant scene in the life of Michal takes place as David brings the Ark of the Lord into Jerusalem. David had taken Jerusalem from the Jebusites and made it the capital of his kingdom. He had wanted to bring the Ark of the Lord into Jerusalem at once, in order that Jerusalem might become the center of the worship of the Lord. Because of the death of Uzzah (2 Samuel 6:1-7), he had abandoned for a time his effort to place the Ark of the Lord in the tabernacle in Jerusalem which he had prepared for it. But now his undertaking receives the blessing of the Lord. When we meditate on the way in which the worship of the Lord later became associated in the life of Israel with the center of this worship in Jerusalem, we can see the full significance of the occasion of David's bringing the Ark of the Lord into the city.

When the Ark comes into Jerusalem, David is moved with a tremendous feeling of enthusiasm and joy as he worships the Lord his God. To express his deep religious emotion David takes off his royal robes, clothes himself with a linen ephod, the dress of a priest, and dances before the Lord at the head of the procession. We need to understand the dance of David. We have here the dance as the means of expressing and communicating to others deep and significant religious feeling. The dance was used in this way in most of the religions of the ancient world. David was great in many ways. He was a leader of men in battle. He could play on a harp and sing in such a way that he is known as the sweet psalmist of Israel. And he could lead a religious dance as an acceptable part of the worship of the Lord. A great dancer was once asked the meaning of her dance. She replied: "Do you think that if I could have said it I would have danced it?" David was expressing through his dance his deepest feelings in the worship of the Lord. And he was able to communicate his meaning to those who participated with him in the procession.

Michal had not joined the joyous company that was bringing the Ark of the Lord into the city. Saul, her father, had never shown any interest in the Ark as the symbol of the worship of the Lord. Michal stayed at home. But she did look out of her window as the procession was approaching. To her amazement she saw David, his royal robes laid aside, dressed in the attire of a priest. She saw him leaping and dancing before the Lord. And she despised him in her heart.

We do not know just what it was that had brought the woman who at one time had loved David to the place at which she despised him. We do know that at this time Michal's marriage died at its heart. A man cannot live in the deepest intimacy of marriage with a woman who despises him. And Michal's scorn of David was not because of the things in him that could rightly be condemned but because of that which represented the noblest part of his life. She had not been interested in the bringing of the

Ark of the Lord to Jerusalem. And she was quite unable to enter into the feelings of David in his worship of the Lord. Michal becomes an example of a woman who cannot or will not enter into the deepest religious experiences of her husband. When David had brought the Ark to its resting place and had offered sacrifices and blessed the people in the name of the Lord, he set his face toward his home with the expectation of blessing his household. But before he could enter his house, Michal met him. She had gone out to upbraid him for having identified himself with the people in his worship of the Lord. In the scene that follows we have in David the mingling of pride and humility that is appropriate in one who has been chosen of the Lord. David's heart goes out in gratitude to the God who has taken him from the sheepfold and lifted him above the house of Saul and anointed him as king. He is conscious of the destiny that is laid on him as the anointed of the Lord. And before the Lord he is willing to make himself contemptible.

Michal, the proud daughter of Saul, was unable to understand her husband as he humbled himself before the Lord. She could not appreciate either his enthusiasm for the worship of the Lord or his humility before the Lord. And the moment of Michal's upbraiding of her husband was also the moment of her encounter with the Lord. The Lord judged Michal as unworthy to be the mother of the son who was to succeed David on the throne of Israel. It was after she had despised David in her heart and upbraided him for humbling himself before the Lord that the inspired writer could comment: "And Michal the daughter of Saul had no child to the day of her death."

# 17

ABIGAIL—the companion of David's wilderness wanderings

*Scripture Background: 1 Samuel 25; 2 Samuel 3:3*

"Blessed be the LORD, the God of Israel, who sent you this day to meet me! " (1 Samuel 25:32).

The meeting of David with Abigail comes toward the close of the time when David as a fugitive from Saul was hiding in an area which is known as the wilderness of Paran, south of Judah. After this we have the story of David and Abishai in the camp of Saul in the wilderness of Ziph. And in the next chapter David decides to seek the protection of the Philistines and is settled by Achish in Ziklag, a village in the extreme south of Judah which was at this time controlled by the Philistines.

The background of the story is the problem of maintaining a guerilla band in a wilderness area. David had with him at the time a band of six hundred men. They had become hardened and disciplined soldiers and are known as one of the great fighting units of history. In addition, these men had begun to gather to them their wives and children. There probably was not very much of this until David was settled at Ziklag, as the life of the fugitive in the desert is not designed for women and children. Over a period of time it would require a large amount of food to furnish provisions for six hundred men. The fugitive cannot stay in one place long enough to plant crops and raise food for himself and those dependent upon him. He cannot turn to the life of the shepherd as he must be ready at any time to flee and leave behind him all that he has. The fugitive from a king who stays within the territory which is even nominally controlled by the king must depend for his support on gifts from his friends. This, of course, can be dangerous business if discovered by the king. Saul slaughtered the priests at Nob because Ahimelech had given provisions to David (1 Samuel 22:11-19).

David's situation was complicated by the fact that he was a fugitive from Saul but was not at war with the men of Israel or of Judah. In this situation David and his men must have received consistent help from their friends in order to remain together as a disciplined army. There were times when David came to the help of his people, as when he rescued the city of Keilah from the Philistines. But in spite of their gratitude to David, the men of Keilah did not dare to offer him protection against Saul (1 Samuel 23:1-14).

David and his men could and did furnish protection to such men as Nabal when their flocks and herds were scattered over wide areas of the wilderness. As the flocks were scattered for pasture, they were constantly exposed to the attacks of marauding bands of desert tribes. But these bands could not operate in an area in which David and his men were hiding. The servants of Nabal pay a tribute to the discipline of David's army when they say to Abigail, "The men were very good to us, and we suffered no harm, and we did not miss anything when we were in the fields, as long as we went with them; they were a wall to us both by night and by day, all the while we were with them keeping the sheep" (1 Samuel 25:15-16). Later when David and his men were settled at Ziklag he had no scruples against attacking the desert tribes to the far south of Judah. In this he considered himself at war with the traditional enemies of Judah (1 Samuel 27:8-12). There may have been times when he demanded "protection money," but David never permitted himself to become a bandit preying upon his own people. Abigail recognizes David's reputation at this time in his life as she says to him, "My lord is fighting the battles of the LORD; and evil shall not be found in you so long as you live" (1 Samuel 25:28). The time when David almost became a robber raiding his own people was in his experience with Nabal.

Nabal belonged to the tribe of Judah and to the family of Caleb. His ancestor Caleb will be remembered as the representative of Judah among the twelve spies who entered the land of Canaan while Israel under Moses was encamped at Kadesh-barnea (Numbers 13:1-6). It was Caleb who along with Joshua insisted that the children of Israel, with the help of their God, were well able to possess the land. Forty years later, following the conquest of the land as a whole, Caleb conquered for himself and his descendants Hebron and the land to the south and east of Hebron. It was in this hill country that Nabal lived. Nabal was a very rich man in a land in which most of the people were poor. His wealth was expressed in terms of flocks and herds. He had three thousand sheep and a thousand goats. Nabal himself is described as churlish and ill-behaved. His servants say of him, "He is so ill-natured that one cannot speak to him" (1 Samuel 25:17).

Abigail was the wife of Nabal. We are told that she was a woman of good understanding and beautiful. In the story before us she lives up to this description. Later, when David woos her for his wife after the death of Nabal, she does not hesitate to leave her secure position as the mistress of a great estate to share with David the life of a fugitive from Saul in the wilderness of Paran. She must have wondered if she had chosen wisely when she was carried captive from Ziklag by a raiding party of Amalekites while David and his men were with the Philistines at the time of the battle of Gilboa. David rescued her from the Amalekites, and she was with him when he went to Hebron to become king of Judah. Her son, Chileab, was the second of the sons of David. However, neither he nor his mother is mentioned in the biblical narrative after the brief reference to them in 2 Samuel 3:3.

When we realize what must have been at times the desperate

need of David and his men for food to sustain life as they were hiding in the wilderness of Paran, we can understand the request for a gift of provisions from Nabal. David sends a request for help which in the thinking of Nabal's men is justified by the protection they have received from David's followers. The ten men whom David sends come at the time of the sheep shearing. This was more than a time for the annual shearing of sheep in the spring. It was often made a festival occasion in which a great abundance of food was prepared for a time of feasting. We can imagine the attractiveness of this abundance of food to hungry men from the desert. To David's carefully framed request for food for his men, Nabal answers: "Who is David? Who is the son of Jesse? There are many servants nowadays who are breaking away from their masters. Shall I take my bread and my water and my meat that I have killed for my shearers, and give it to men who come from I do not know where?" (1 Samuel 25:11).

When David received the answer of Nabal, he said to his men, "Every man gird on his sword!" (1 Samuel 25:13). We can understand David's feelings as he received the insulting reply of Nabal, but we cannot excuse his reaction to it in setting forth on an expedition in which his announced purpose was to destroy Nabal and his house and to seize for himself the food which Nabal had refused to give. If he had carried out his purpose this deed of wrath would have been forever a blot on his name, and if David and his men had continued in this fashion they might have become the scourge of Judah instead of the men who were fighting the battles of the Lord. And they would have known bloodguiltiness, the knowledge that they were guilty before God for having shed the blood of innocent people.

The person who saved David from this deed of shame was Abigail. We must admire this woman for the speed with which she acts when she learns from her servants of the evil that is intended against her husband's house. We must admire her for the courage with which she goes out without the knowledge of her husband to face a band of four hundred armed men. Her speech to David is carefully phrased as she recalls him to his better self.

The significant thing about this meeting of David and Abigail is that David feels that Abigail is sent of the Lord to save him from the crime which he had almost committed. He says to her, "Blessed be the LORD, the God of Israel, who sent you this day to meet me! Blessed be your discretion, and blessed be you, who have kept me this day from bloodguilt and from avenging myself with my own hand!" (1 Samuel 25: 32-33).

There emerges here a concept of God as One who is interested in us as individuals and as One who may come to us through another individual whom he has sent to us to save us from a sinful deed. David's encounter with Abigail was also his encounter with the Lord, the God of Israel. We are not surprised that later, when Nabal has died of a stroke, David wants to marry the woman who as the messenger of God had come to him in his time of wrath and saved him from a deed in which he would have been guilty before God. To many a man, in times of decision and wrath, God has come through the quiet voice of his wife as she urged him to restraint and insisted that he leave vengeance to God.

The concept of God which we have here is found also in the psalms of David. God to David is not some faraway person who is only remotely interested in human life. David can write, "The LORD is my shepherd . . . He leads me in paths of righteousness." Perhaps when David wrote this he was thinking of the time the Lord came to him through Abigail and led him in the paths of righteousness when in his wrath he stood on the brink of a deed of vengeance.

The concept of God which underlies this story is in agreement with what Jesus has taught us about God. He says to us: "Are not two sparrows sold for a penny? And not one of them will fall to the ground without your Father's will. But even the hairs of your head are all numbered. Fear not, therefore; you are of more value than many sparrows" (Matthew 10:29-31). Jesus pictures for us the joy before the angels of God over one sinner who repents (Luke 15:10). He himself prays for Simon that his faith may not fail (Luke 22:31-32). The God who has made himself known to us in the Bible is the God who is interested in every human being and is seeking to lead each of us in the paths of righteousness. He comes to us today as he came to David through Abigail, to save us from presumptuous sins and to lead us into his purpose for us.

# 18

## BATHSHEBA—wife of Uriah and mother of Solomon

*Scripture Background: 2 Samuel 11:1—12:25; 1 Kings 1; 2:13-25*

"The LORD also has put away your sin" (2 Samuel 12:13).

Bathsheba is the woman whom David loved more deeply than any other woman who entered his life. It was to satisfy his desire for Bathsheba that David despised the word of the Lord and committed the sin of adultery. But Bathsheba became the intimate companion of David during his mature years and the mother of the son who succeeded him on the throne.

Bathsheba was the daughter of Eliam and the wife of Uriah the Hittite. We do not know the story of how this woman of Israel met and married Uriah, a man of the Hittites. We would judge from his inclusion in the number of David's mighty men that Uriah was a man of great physical strength and of unusual skill in the handling of the weapons of war. It may have been this side of his life that first attracted the attention of the beautiful Bathsheba. He was drawn to her by her beauty, and she admired him for his strength. We know, also, that in spite of his Hittite background Uriah himself was a worshiper of the God of Israel. Bathsheba did not in any way compromise her religious faith when she married Uriah.

After the conquest of Jerusalem, Uriah and Bathsheba moved into a house in Jerusalem that was close to the king's palace. Uriah's house, like most of the other houses of the time, had a flat roof, and the roof of his house was clearly visible from the roof of the king's house. Uriah and Bathsheba lived together in Jerusalem until in the spring of the year Uriah was sent with an expedition under the command of Joab to carry on the war with the Ammonites. Bathsheba's first contact with David was when David became aware of her beauty while he was walking on the roof of his house in the late afternoon. David inquired who the woman was and learned that she was the wife of Uriah the Hittite. It was at this point that David should have called a halt to his interest in the beautiful woman he had seen. But instead David sent messengers to her and invited her to come to his house.

Rembrandt has a well-known painting of Bathsheba. He used his great skill as a painter to depict the body of a very beautiful woman. In this painting Bathsheba is holding a letter in her hand. It is the letter from the king inviting her to come to him. As we look upon the face of Bathsheba as Rembrandt has painted her we know that we are looking upon a woman who was one of the most beautiful women of her time. But Rembrandt has also pictured the face of a woman who is tortured with a great decision. As Bathsheba holds the letter of the king in her hand she is torn between her loyalty to her husband and her desire to accept the invitation of the king.

The life of David would have been very different if Bathsheba had resisted the temptation to have an affair with David and had saved the king from the sin that did so much to wreck his life, his home, and his kingdom. Bathsheba, like Abigail, might have come to David as one sent of the Lord to recall him to his true self. But Bathsheba was flattered by the attention of the king. She went to David and gave herself to him.

Bathsheba returned to her own home. In time she found that she was with child. Only those who have been in similar circumstances can understand fully the conflicting emotions which Bathsheba must have experienced. There was in her, as in all women, the yearning for the experience of motherhood. But she knew that when it became evident that she had become pregnant while her husband, Uriah, was away in the war with the Ammonites, she would be in danger of being put to death. This was the stern law of the land of Israel (Leviticus 20:10). In this situation, Bathsheba had no choice but to send to David the message, "I am with child" (2 Samuel 11:5).

We do not know how deeply Bathsheba was involved in the things that went on after David received her message. She can hardly have been ignorant of the time that Uriah came to Jerusalem as the messenger of Joab to David. Who can imagine the painful agitation which Bathsheba experienced as she waited for two days for the husband who did not come to her? She probably was aware of how Uriah felt about the code of the soldier who was involved in an expedition. But after Uriah returned to duty with the army she knew that nothing had been done to protect her in the time when it would become known that she was with child.

The probability is that Bathsheba was not aware of the written message that David sent to Joab by the hand of Uriah. But when almost immediately the news came of Uriah's death, Bathsheba must have wondered if there had been foul play involved in the death of her husband in the battle with the Ammonites. Regardless of what her suspicions may have been, Bathsheba went through a period of mourning for her husband. As soon as the time of lamentation was over, David sent for Bathsheba and brought her to his home and she became his wife. In due time she gave birth to a son, and although there may have been some talk about the palace, there was no one who dared to accuse her openly.

The story of David and Bathsheba might have ended with a secret that was never brought out into the open if it had not been for the visit to David of Nathan the prophet. It was in this visit that David and Bathsheba saw themselves not in the eyes of man but in the eyes of God. It was here that they saw the full gravity of their sin. And the sin of Bathsheba must not be minimized. She was as guilty as the guilty queen in *Hamlet*. And the judgment in which the death of her son was predicted must have cut Bathsheba to the core.

We are not told the reactions of Bathsheba to the visit of Nathan. But we probably are justified in assuming that Bathsheba passed through an experience of deep repentance for sin and of realized forgiveness in which she came to the knowledge that the Lord had put away her sin. There are various indications of this. Bathsheba remained throughout the rest of her life the most beloved of the wives of David. She would not have been spiritually qualified for this kind of fellowship with David if she had not known both repentance and the assurance of the forgiveness of her God. Bathsheba from this time on seems to have been closely associated with Nathan. This dependence upon Nathan the prophet as her spiritual adviser would not have been possible if Bathsheba had not experienced repentance and forgiveness. The blessing of the Lord seems to have rested on the choice of Bathsheba's son, Solomon, to succeed David on the throne. In the opening chapter of Matthew, we find Bathsheba mentioned along with Ruth the Moabite and Rahab the harlot in the genealogy of Jesus Christ.

Bathsheba was a woman who was unquestionably guilty of adultery. She also was a woman who repented and was forgiven. In spite of her sin, she proved herself worthy of an honored place as wife of David, mother of Solomon, and queen of Israel.

The story of Bathsheba after the visit of Nathan is not told in detail. She shared with David the judgments of God which were part of the retribution which had to come to David as a consequence of his sin. In particular she faced with David the sickness and death of their son. We can be sure that she shared with David his grief and his prayer for the life of the child. We can be sure, too, that she accepted the death of her son without bitterness as part of the judgment of God for a sin in which she and David had utterly scorned the word of the Lord. We can hope that she entered with David into the hope of a reunion beyond death with the son who had gone from her.

In time Bathsheba gave birth to a second son, who was named Solomon. She seems to have committed some of his training to Nathan the prophet. It may be that part of the wisdom of Solomon came through the things he learned from his mother. Bathsheba's greatest impact upon her world was in the training of the man who was to rule for forty years over all Israel.

It is reasonable to suppose that Bathsheba and her son fled from Jerusalem at the time of Absalom's rebellion. When Joab rebuked David for his grief over Absalom, he said to him: "You have today covered with shame the faces of all your servants, who have this day saved your life, and the lives of your sons and daughters, and the lives of your wives and your concubines" (2 Samuel 19:5). It is clear that Joab felt that the victory of Absalom would have meant the death of both Bathsheba and Solomon.

In later years, when it became obvious that David was near to death, Bathsheba played an active part in the events leading to the establishment of her son, Solomon, on the throne of Israel. David had sworn to her by the Lord, saying, "Solomon your son shall reign after me, and he shall sit upon my throne" (1 Kings 1:17). But while David intended for Solomon to succeed him he was making no effort to establish Solomon on the throne during his lifetime. In the meantime, Adonijah, the fourth son of David, had won the allegiance of Joab, commander of the army, and Abiathar the priest, and had had himself crowned king without the knowledge of David. Adonijah had not included among the guests at the crowning Nathan the prophet, or Zadok the priest, or Benaiah the son of Jehoiada, captain of David's bodyguard, or Solomon. Nathan heard of the conspiracy and knew that the lives of both Bathsheba and Solomon were in great danger. It was a situation which required quick and vigorous action, and Bathsheba and Nathan were able to arouse the aged David to the urgency of the situation. Knowing that he must act at once, David arranged to have Solomon crowned by Zadok and Nathan. He gave him also the support of his bodyguard under the command of Benaiah, the son of Jehoiada. Solomon was established on the throne and Bathsheba was safe. Our last look at Bathsheba is when she innocently agrees to ask her son Solomon to give to Adonijah as his wife Abishag the Shunammite, the beautiful maiden who had ministered to David in his last illness. Solomon was probably correct in interpreting this as a second attempt at the throne and in ordering the execution of Adonijah.

We could wish that David had never sinned in the matter of the adultery with Bathsheba and the murder of Uriah, but we can be glad that God while he moved in judgment moved also in mercy and in forgiveness. We find in Bathsheba an example of a woman who was guilty of great sin but who repented of her sin and received forgiveness, finally proving herself worthy of a place of honor in the life of a nation.

# 19

## THE SON OF BATHSHEBA—who died in infancy

*Scripture Background: 2 Samuel 12:1-23*

"I shall go to him, but he will not return to me" (2 Samuel 12:23).

A man and a woman stand together and watch the cradle of a baby boy who is desperately ill. The man is David, king of Israel. The woman is Bathsheba, one of the most beautiful women in Israel, formerly the wife of Uriah the Hittite, now the wife of David. The baby boy is their son, the child of adultery. As Bathsheba watches her son in an illness that has all the marks of a sickness unto death, she remembers the time when she was first sure of his coming and was forced to send David the message: "I am with child" (2 Samuel 11:5). As David watches, he remembers the way in which he had sought to cover their sin by having Uriah sent back to Jerusalem. And he remembers that when this failed he wrote to Joab: "Set Uriah in the forefront of the hardest fighting, and then draw back from him, that he may be struck down, and die" (2 Samuel 11:15). He remembers also the message he received from Joab: "Your servant Uriah the Hittite is dead also" (2 Samuel 11:21). Both David and Bathsheba know that "the thing that David had done displeased the LORD" (2 Samuel 11:27). And they cannot have forgotten the words of Nathan the prophet: "Because by this deed you have utterly scorned the LORD, the child that is born to you shall die" (2 Samuel 12:14). They know that the sickness of their son is a sickness unto death as part of the judgment of God on their sin.

As David and Bathsheba face the sickness of their son, they face it as those who have received the forgiveness of God. We do not have a record of the inner experiences of Bathsheba, but it is fair to assume that when confronted by the word of the Lord through Nathan the prophet she shared with David his repentance and his confession of sin and received with him the word of pardon. From this time on, Bathsheba is established as the wife of David and the queen of Israel. We do know that when Nathan confronted him with the word of the Lord in the matter of Uriah the Hittite, David said: "I have sinned against the LORD" (2 Samuel 12:13). These are simple words; they can be said with little depth of meaning. Saul was always ready to confess that he had sinned against the Lord yet was never ready to change his manner of living. But the repentance of David was a soul-searching experience. We cannot be perfectly sure that the great penitential Psalms in the form in which we now have them were written by David, but they express the kind of experience that David passed through when he turned from his sin unto God, and the Thirty-second and Fifty-first Psalms should be read in this setting. After David's repentance, Nathan was able to say to him: "The LORD also has put away your sin; you shall not die" (2 Samuel 12:13).

David had received the forgiveness of God. He could realize again the sense of God's presence with him. He could go to God in prayer without having the reality of unrepented sin rise before him. But while forgiveness does mean the restoration of our relation to God, it does not mean the blotting out of all the consequences of sin. David still had to face in Amnon's sin and Absalom's rebellion the working out of the consequences of his own sin. When a child in a home sins, the parents may speak the word of forgiveness and the broken relation between parents and child may be restored. But it may be necessary to face over a period of years the consequences of that sin.

The heart of David's sin was that in it he had despised the word of the Lord. Or, as Nathan says, he had "utterly scorned the LORD." And it was to David after he had received forgiveness that the word was spoken: "The child that is born to you shall die" (2 Samuel 12:14). We cannot enter into this divine decision. We can, of course, suggest some reasons why a judgment of this kind was necessary. But this was God's decision; and, as with many other decisions of God, we must accept it in the certainty that it is the decision of One who does not needlessly afflict the children of men.

We can enter into David's suffering as he looks upon his infant son who is sick unto death. Part of the greatness of David is his capacity to feel—his ability to experience significant suffering. It has been said of Kierkegaard that his amazing capacity to feel was the key to much of his greatest writing. He interpreted the meaning of his suffering. In this scene and in his suffering over the death of Absalom, David reveals himself to us as a man who has tremendous capacity for feeling. As David perceives the full meaning of the sickness of his infant son, he casts himself upon the earth. He refuses to take food. He is not ashamed of weeping. He refuses to heed those who try to lift him up. He remains overcome by grief for a period of seven days.

In this experience of grief and suffering, David faced encounter with God in terms of judgment. He had despised the word of the Lord and he had violated the moral order which grounds in the will of God. He had thought that he could mock God and get by with it. He had to learn that no man mocks God and that no man sins with impunity. But we are not to think that every sickness of a loved one comes to us in terms of judgment. We need to remember the words of Jesus concerning the man born blind: "It was not that this man sinned, or his parents . . ." (John 9:2). These experiences can come to us, however, as part of the discipline of life that God has set for us.

David's time of fasting and weeping was also a time of intercessory prayer. As he interpreted his actions to his servants after the death of the child, he said: "While the child was still alive, I fasted and wept; for I said, 'Who knows whether the LORD will be gracious to me, that the child may live?' " David was dealing here not with some impersonal fate but with the living Lord. The God of David is able to show mercy and to alter his judgments. When Elijah pronounced the judgment of God on

Ahab because of the death of Naboth, Ahab humbled himself and "went softly" all his days (1 Kings 21:27, K.J.V.). And because Ahab had humbled himself the Lord altered his judgment and postponed the things spoken through Elijah until after the death of Ahab (1 Kings 21:29). But David's prayer for the life of his son was not granted. At the end of seven days, the child died.

David accepted the finality of death. He knew that his son could not come back to him. He accepted the judgment of the Lord without bitterness as he went from his time of weeping and fasting into the house of the Lord to worship. The Lord did not answer David's prayer for the life of his son, but he did give to David in his time of grief an insight into the life beyond death which was unique at this time in the history of Israel. As he thought of his son who was dead, David said: *"I shall go to him"* (2 Samuel 12:23).

In this David moved beyond the faith of most of his contemporaries. Hebrew religion in the time of David was of the earth, earthy. The judgments of God and the blessings of communion with God were thought to be experienced only in this life. But David knew that while his son could not come to him, he would go to be with his son. This involved first of all the belief that for his infant son death did not mean annihilation but the continuation of life in a world beyond death. David probably did not think through the full meaning of this, but at least he knew that his child whose life was cut short at the end of a few weeks was with the Lord and that with the Lord he would grow and develop so that he would be a living person when the time came for David to pass into the great beyond. David's faith must also have included his own hope of surviving the crisis of death and the belief that in the world beyond death he would be able to recognize his son when he met him.

We see here parenthood in a dimension of depth that is possible only in the light of faith in God. When David and Bathsheba united in the bringing of this child into the world they were permitted under God not only to give birth to a tiny body that lived a few weeks and died; they brought into being a little baby who had a soul that would survive death. After their earthly pilgrimage, David and Bathsheba would stand in the presence of this child and their child would know that in the providence of God these two had given him being. In this sense man, woman, and child are set in a trinity of being that is irrevocable. We cannot be sure that David understood all of this, but we can know that he expected, at the end of his earthly pilgrimage, to go and be with his son.

As we meditate on this story, we realize afresh the tremendous difference that Jesus Christ makes. He has opened to us the things that David in his grief only dimly grasped. Jesus has passed through death and has come back to witness to us of the resurrection world of God that is beyond death. He has told us of the many mansions that are in the Father's house. He has told us that he has gone to prepare a place for us and that he will come again to receive us into the heavenly home (John 14:1-7). Because of Jesus, millions of parents who also have faced the death of a little baby have known that in Jesus' keeping their child was safe. They have lived out their earthly pilgrimage in the hope of being reunited with the child that was taken from them. In Christ, the hope that David laid hold of in his time of grief has become the assured faith of the people of God.

# 20

AMNON—the terrible cost of illicit sexual adventure

*Scripture Background: 2 Samuel 13*

"This is the will of God . . . that you abstain from immorality" (1 Thessalonians 4:3).
"Walk by the Spirit, and do not gratify the desires of the flesh" (Galatians 5:16).

As we read the story of Amnon we must realize David's involvement in the sin of his son. David's failure to control his sexual desires rendered him unfit to lead his sons in the way of purity. But the sons of David were responsible for their sinful choices. They could not blame their violations of the law of God on the failure of their father.

Amnon was the firstborn son of David. His mother was Ahinoam of Jezreel whom David took as his wife, along with Abigail the widow of Nabal, while he was still a fugitive from Saul. Both wives were carried captive by the Amalekites when they attacked Ziklag at the time of the battle of Gilboa. David rescued Ahinoam and Abigail by his successful pursuit of the raiders. Amnon was not born until after David was established at Hebron as king over Judah.

As the firstborn son of David, Amnon had the right to expect to follow his father on the throne of Israel. When we think of the glory of Solomon we can understand something of the heritage that might have come to Amnon. As son of David, born during the days when the young David was walking in the way of the Lord, Amnon must have entered into some understanding of the faith that gave meaning to the life of his father. Through his association with his father he certainly knew the peculiar obligation that rested upon the king as the anointed of the Lord to walk in obedience to the word of the Lord.

Amnon formed a guilty love for his half-sister, Tamar. She was the daughter of David and Maacah, the daughter of Talmai king of Geshur. She was the full sister of Absalom. Tamar was a beautiful and spirited woman, and Amnon looked upon her with lustful eyes. Of course there stood between Amnon and Tamar the fact that as she was his sister he could not expect to take her as his wife. Perhaps the most universal of all the customs concerning marriage is the prohibition of marriage between brothers and sisters. It was strictly forbidden in the law of Israel (Leviticus 20:17). In the midst of her humiliation Tamar said to Amnon: "I pray you, speak to the king; for he will not withhold me from you." But in her heart Tamar knew, and Amnon knew, that the king would not give Amnon permission to take his sister as his wife. They knew, too, that even if the king gave his permission, the people of Israel would not tolerate it. The desire of Amnon for Tamar was not the pure love of a man who seeks a woman for his wife. It was the lustful desire of a man who seeks to gratify his own sexual desires.

We can understand, if we do not excuse, the way in which lustful thoughts came to Amnon as he looked upon the beautiful Tamar. Amnon's first mistake was in letting those thoughts stay with him. He lived with them in the realm of his imagination until he "was so tormented that he made himself ill because of his sister Tamar" (2 Samuel 13:2). There is a proverb that says we cannot prevent birds from flying over our heads but we do not have to let them make nests in our hair. Amnon needed to learn that the battleground of the struggle for purity is first of all in the realm of the imagination.

During the time that he was looking lustfully at Tamar there was a moral struggle going on in the life of Amnon. It was a time in which he knew himself to be confronted with the will of God. In the life of Israel, the demand for purity was always given as the command of God. Joseph when he was tempted by Potiphar's wife cried out: "How then can I do this great wickedness, and sin against God?" (Genesis 39:9). And Nathan when he came to David in condemnation of his sin with Bathsheba said: "Why have you *despised the word of the Lord,* to do what is evil in his sight? You have smitten Uriah the Hittite with the sword, and have taken his wife to be your wife" (2 Samuel 12:9). He went on to say: "By this deed you have utterly scorned the LORD" (2 Samuel 12:14). And David in his great penitential psalm said to the Lord: "Against thee, thee only, have I sinned, and done that which is evil in thy sight" (Psalm 51:4). Amnon knew that the violation of the seventh commandment was the violation of the moral order which is an expression of the will of God.

The biblical writers do not condemn sexual desire as in itself sinful. They give no support to the idea that it is possible to attain in the life of celibacy a degree of holiness that is not possible in the married life. What they do condemn is the refusal of man to accept the law of the Lord as setting the pattern within which it is right to give creative expression to sexual desire. They know that it is not good for man to be alone and that it is the purpose of God that man and woman shall find within the marriage relation a unity upon which his blessing can rest. They protect the sanctity of the home by condemning both fornication and adultery.

Amnon faced, as many another man has faced, the struggle between the moral and the sexual. The full intensity of the struggle that went on within his soul is revealed by the way in which after his lust was satisfied his love turned to hate. We are told that Amnon hated Tamar with a very great hatred, "so that the hatred with which he hated her was greater than the love with which he had loved her" (2 Samuel 13:15). When his deed of shame was finished, Amnon could not abide Tamar in his presence because she became to him the symbol of the violation he had done to his whole moral nature and of his guilt before God.

The probability is that Amnon would never have translated into action his guilty love for Tamar if he had not been spurred on by his friend Jonadab, the son of Shimeah, David's brother. This man, who was Amnon's first cousin, is the most despicable character in the whole sordid story of the rape of Tamar. He was an evil and crafty man who helped another man achieve his wicked desire. Amnon revealed his own character in that he had made an intimate friend of such a man as Jonadab. Jonadab pretended to be helping Ammon, but he led him to a course that brought about his ruin. And while it is not expressly stated, the suggestion is that later Jonadab plotted with Absalom the manner in which Absalom avenged the wrong to Tamar with the death of Amnon. It is clear that Jonadab knew in advance of the return of the king's sons that Amnon only was to be slain (2 Samuel 13:32). But the evil influence of Jonadab over him was no excuse for the conduct of Amnon. Amnon acted as a responsible person who was dominated by his physical desires and wrecked the life of his sister Tamar.

Amnon paid a terrible price for a few moments of sexual satisfaction. He was the heir apparent to the throne. He should have become the Lord's anointed to follow his father in establishing a throne through which the rule of God would be expressed in the life of Israel. But after this scene it must have been evident to David and to all Israel that Amnon was not the man who could establish the throne with righteousness and justice.

Amnon had to live with the knowledge of the wrong he had done to Tamar. When Absalom comforted Tamar he said to her, "Has Amnon your brother been with you? Now hold your peace, my sister; he is your brother; do not take this to heart." But Tamar did not regard lightly the wrong she had received. She tore up the robe that was the token of her virginity, put ashes on her head, and walked weeping from the house of Amnon. And Absalom showed that he did take this thing to heart when he voluntarily went into exile as the consequence of having carried through the murder of Amnon.

When the story of what Amnon had done was told to his father, David was very angry. Yet he did not move to discipline Amnon. It was David's failure to discipline his son that doubtless gave Absalom the feeling that he had the right to take vengeance into his own hands. But something had come between Amnon and his father that would not pass away. Amnon had destroyed his father's trust in him, and David suffered through his knowledge of the evil that was in the heart of his eldest son. Amnon had to live with himself. Before his sin he lived through a period of tension in which a struggle went on in his soul between the moral and the sexual. The intensity of his struggle shows that he was not all bad. But he permitted his lust to lead him to violate his sense of right and wrong. In so doing, instead of finding peace he entered into an experience of guilt and remorse. In this he probably suffered more than he had suffered during the time when he was tormented by his guilty passion for Tamar. But so far as we know, with Amnon remorse never led to repentance, confession, and forgiveness. He never restored the broken relationships, and when Absalom strikes him down we feel the sheer tragedy of a man who has wrecked his life through his failure to discipline his sexual life in the light of his knowledge of the will of the Lord.

The story of Amnon needs to be set in the dimensions of the Christian faith. When Paul wrote to the Thessalonians he found it necessary to make clear to the Christians at Thessalonica the demand for purity in the sexual life that is at the heart of the Christian faith. He does this in 1 Thessalonians 4:1-8. He reminds the Thessalonians that the things he is saying in this letter are a summary of the instructions he has already given them through the Lord Jesus. He proceeds to tell them that the will of God for them is that they abstain from immorality. He says that a Christian man is to "know how to take a wife for himself in holiness and honor, not in the passion of lust like heathen who do not know God" (1 Thessalonians 4:4-5). The trouble with Amnon was that he acted in passion and lust and not in holiness and honor. Paul says that at the heart of the sins of sex there is a wrong to persons. Amnon did a great wrong to his father, to his brothers, and to his sister. Paul writes to the Thessalonians: "The Lord is an avenger in all these things, as we solemnly forewarned you." Amnon found, as all others will find, that he could not violate the command of God and avoid the judgment of God.

Paul concludes by reminding the Thessalonians that God has called them to holiness and has given his Holy Spirit to help them. God calls us to holiness. He calls us to purity in the sexual life. But he does not call us to an impossible demand. He gives his Holy Spirit to us, and if we will walk by the promptings of the Spirit we will not fulfill the lusts of the flesh.

# 21

ABSALOM—rebellious son of an undisciplined father

*Scripture Background: 2 Samuel 3:2-5; 13:1—19:15*

"God . . . doth . . . devise means, that his banished be not expelled from him" (2 Samuel 14:14, K.J.V.).

The biblical narrative of Absalom's rebellion, with its climax in the grief of David for his son, is one of the great stories of literature. It is difficult to find in either ancient or modern literature a more masterful piece of writing than this portion of Second Samuel. But we are interested in it not for its literary excellence but for its revelation of David and Absalom in their encounter with God.

There is a very real sense in which David was in part responsible for the trouble he had with his sons. It was because of David's failure to discipline himself that he proved unable to discipline his sons. There is the familiar but true saying that we teach by what we say, more by what we do, and most by what we are. When David became involved in the adultery with Bathsheba and in the murder of Uriah he compromised himself in such a way that he was no longer able to command the respect and obedience of his sons.

We need to realize that the trouble which arose in David's family was a fulfillment of the word of the Lord through Nathan the prophet. Nathan had said to David: "Thus says the LORD, 'Behold, I will raise up evil against you out of *your own house*" (2 Samuel 12:11). It is characteristic of the writer of Second Samuel that he recognizes the judgments of the Lord not so much in supernatural events as in events which arise out of the context of the life of the world in which we live. The Lord moves in mercy and in judgment as he rules and over-rules the things that men do as they move in accordance with their own sinful desires. This is one of the things that makes the narratives of Second Samuel so relevant to life today.

Absalom was the third son of David. Amnon was the first. Chileab, the son of Abigail the widow of Nabal of Carmel, was second. But for some reason he drops out of the narrative. The probability is that he did not live to maturity. When Absalom killed Amnon in revenge for the rape of his sister Tamar, the way was opened for Absalom to stand first in the line of the succession.

So far as his physical appearance was concerned, the young Absalom was a perfect example of physical strength and beauty. We are told that from the sole of his foot to the crown of his head there was no blemish in him. He was particularly proud of his hair. He wore it long in order that he might display it, and when he cut it once a year it weighed two hundred shekels. As we compare the young Absalom with the young David we should remember the word spoken at the time of the anointing of David: "The LORD sees not as man sees; man looks on the outward appearance, but the LORD looks on the heart" (1 Samuel 16:7). It could never have been said that Absalom was a man after God's own heart.

According to 2 Samuel 14:27, "There were born to Absalom three sons, and one daughter whose name was Tamar; she was a beautiful woman." We have some difficulty in harmonizing this with the story told in 2 Samuel 18:18, that Absalom had set up a pillar for himself in the King's Valley, saying, "I have no son to keep my name in remembrance." The monument may have been set up before the birth of his sons, or his sons may have perished in some tragedy unknown to us.

The young Absalom must have been a most attractive man. He was able to steal the hearts of all Israel, and his father loved him with that deep capacity for significant feeling which is characteristic of David. But the young Absalom was not a good man. We can understand his feelings toward Amnon and his concern to avenge the wrong done to Tamar, but Absalom had no right to take vengeance into his own hands and to become guilty of his brother's blood to avenge his sister's honor. And Absalom's rebellion was not a deed done in the heat of passion. He plotted his rebellion over a period of years. In order to seize the throne for himself, Absalom was willing to kill the father who had recalled him from banishment. In his effort to seize the crown, he plunged Israel into a civil war in which twenty thousand men died in one battle. The moral enormity of Absalom's sin should not be played down.

From the sin of Absalom we turn to the sorrow of David. We can be sure that at first David's reaction to the treachery of Absalom was that of wrath. If Absalom had overtaken his father as he fled from Jerusalem, he would probably have found in David a man of war who knew how to use a sword. The fleeing David recognized this rebellion as part of the judgment of God on him in his sin against Uriah the Hittite, but this did not change his feeling concerning his own son who sought his father's life.

As David gathered his forces and prepared for battle he was torn between his love for his son and his concern for his throne and for the safety of the loyal men who stood with him. When the battle was about to be joined, David offered to lead his soldiers in battle as he did in the days of his youth. Joab refused to permit this, as he knew full well that the death of David would leave David's army with nothing to fight for. David had to wait in the city to hear the news of the battle. In the long period of waiting his heart was torn between his desire for victory and his concern for his son. And in the end, when he knew the battle was over, his fear for his son dominated him. His charge to the people had been: "Deal gently for my sake with the young man Absalom" (2 Samuel 18:5). And his first question to each of the runners was, "Is it well with the young man Absalom?" (2 Samuel 18:29, 32). And when he knew that Absalom was dead, he cried out, "O my son Absalom, my son, my son Absalom! Would I had died instead of you, O Absalom, my son, my son!" (2 Samuel 18:33).

David in his wrath at Absalom's treachery and in his love for his son which persisted in spite of Absalom's faithlessness is an inadequate human example of the heart of God as there is present with God at the same time the divine wrath against sin and the love which persists in spite of the faithlessness of man. Hosea expresses this when the Lord speaks through his prophet, saying:

"When Israel was a child, I loved him,
    and out of Egypt I called my son.
The more I called them,
    the more they went from me;
they kept sacrificing to the Baals,
    and burning incense to idols.

"Yet it was I who taught Ephraim to walk,
    I took them up in my arms;
    but they did not know that I healed them.
. . . . . . . .
"How can I give you up, O Ephraim!
    How can I hand you over, O Israel!
How can I make you like Admah!
    How can I treat you like Zeboiim!
My heart recoils within me,
    my compassion grows warm and tender.
I will not execute my fierce anger,
    I will not again destroy Ephraim;
for I am God and not man,
    the Holy One in your midst,
    and I will not come to destroy" (Hosea 11:1-3, 8-9).

Paul as he discusses the unbelief of Israel quotes the word of the Lord to Isaiah concerning Israel: "All day long I have held out my hands to a disobedient and contrary people" (Romans 10:21).

There was nothing that David in his grief could do for Absalom. Joab was right in knowing that Absalom had to die. David could not die for Absalom. But God can do what man cannot do. God has sent his only begotten Son to die for the sin of man. As the wise woman of Tekoa said to David: "God . . . doth . . . devise means, that his banished be not expelled from him" (2 Samuel 14:14, K.J.V.).

God in Christ has wrought out an atonement in which the sin of man is covered. "God shows his love for us in that while we were yet sinners Christ died for us" (Romans 5:8). The grief of David for Absalom can help us to understand the cost to God the Father when he sends his Son to the cross to make atonement for the sin of man.

# 22

## SOLOMON—the wisdom and the glory and the folly

*Scripture Background: 2 Samuel 12:24-25; 1 Kings 1-11; 1 Chronicles 23:1; 2 Chronicles 1-9*

"When Solomon was old his wives turned away his heart after other gods; and his heart was not wholly true to the LORD his God" (1 Kings 11:4).

Solomon was the second son of David and Bathsheba. It was said of him at his birth that the Lord loved him. He was a man who in his natural endowments was richly gifted. As he grew up in the palace, his life was molded by his contacts with his father, his mother, and the prophet Nathan. Of the sons of David who are known to us, Solomon was easily the best qualified to succeed his father on the throne. David promised Bathsheba that her son should reign after him. We would judge from the activity of Nathan the prophet in bringing about the crowning of Solomon, and also from the words of Adonijah to Bathsheba (1 Kings 2:15), that the blessing of the Lord rested on the choice of Solomon as king. Solomon did not have to fight for his throne. He was placed on the throne by the combined efforts of such people as Nathan, his mother Bathsheba, his father David when he was at last aroused, and the support of Zadok the priest and Benaiah the son of Jehoiada, the commander of David's bodyguard. After the death of David, when Adonijah asked for Abishag the Shunammite as his wife, Solomon was probably right in interpreting the request as the beginning of a second attempt at the throne. It may have been necessary to order the execution of Adonijah, but we cannot but feel that Solomon should have spared Joab in recognition of his age and his services to Israel.

Once he was firmly established on the throne, the young Solomon bore himself wisely as king. His first confrontation with the Lord after he became king was when the Lord appeared to him in a dream at Gibeon and said to him, "Ask what I shall give you." Solomon answered: "Give thy servant . . . an understanding mind to govern thy people, that I may discern between good and evil; for who is able to govern this thy great people?" (1 Kings 3:5-9).

The request for wisdom to govern the people pleased the Lord, and the Lord promised to give to Solomon also riches and honor. In the first years of his reign Solomon lived up to the hopes of those who had made him king. He became known for his understanding and his wisdom. His name has been connected with the book of Proverbs. And while Solomon is certainly not the author of all of this book, he may have played an important part both in uttering and in collecting many proverbs which are a penetrating summary of the practical wisdom of Israel.

David had been a man of war. But the early years of Solomon's reign were a time of profound peace. This meant that Solomon had time to give himself to developing the internal resources of his kingdom and to building up the trade of Israel with the rest of the world. He established a port at Ezion-geber on the Gulf of Aqaba and engaged in extensive trade with parts of the world which up to this time had been unknown to Israel. He also carried on extensive mining operations.

Solomon built the temple of the Lord at Jerusalem. David had made extensive preparations for the building of the temple. But it was under the leadership of Solomon that the temple was actually built. When we think of the place of the temple worship in the life of Israel, we need to remember that the building of the temple was the work of Solomon. For the carrying on of his building operations he entered into an alliance with Hiram, king of Tyre. The cedar for the temple was imported from Lebanon, and skilled workmen from Phoenicia aided the Jews in the actual construction of the temple. The prayer of Solomon at the dedication of the temple is a great prayer. Centuries later when the Jews were in exile they remembered the glory of Solomon's temple.

During the reign of Solomon, the empire of Israel reached its peak in terms of external glory and splendor. Within the land, there was security from internal strife and from foreign invasion. The Jews remembered it as a time when every man could sit under his own vine and his own fig tree and there was none to make them afraid. Jesus shared with the people of his own generation the memory of the glory of Solomon (Matthew 6:29). He showed how little he was affected by this kind of glory as he contrasted the glory of Solomon with the beauty of a lily of the field.

But the glory that was Solomon's proved to be an empty glory. Solomon loved many foreign women. His father, David, had followed the pattern of the kings of his time and had taken unto himself many wives and concubines. Most of David's wives were from the daughters of Israel, but Solomon knew no restraint in the choosing of wives and concubines. He violated the law of the Lord by taking to himself wives who did not worship the God who had made himself known to Israel. It is probably true that many of Solomon's marriages were made to cement his political alliances. But Solomon will always be known as the king with three hundred wives and seven hundred concubines, one man and a thousand women. This was certainly part of the folly and extravagance of Solomon.

"When Solomon was old his wives turned away his heart after other gods; and his heart was not wholly true to the LORD his God, as was the heart of David his father" (1 Kings 11:4). There is about the worship of the Lord an element of intolerance that is born of its claim to be the worship of the one true God. The God who revealed himself to Israel is a jealous God who will not give his glory to another. Solomon began by tolerating the worship of false gods by his wives and concubines. He went on to build in Jerusalem places of worship to false gods. He built altars to Chemosh, the abomination of the Moabites, and to Molech, the abomination of the Ammonites. There was no place in the worship of Israel for a religious syncretism in which the worship of the Lord would be combined with the worship of false gods. But under the patronage of Solomon the detestable idolatries of the nations around about Israel were protected and practiced in Jerusalem along with the worship of the Lord. At the heart of the worship of the Lord there is the capacity to reject ideas that are foreign to it. But Solomon fell into an easygoing religious syncretism in which the worship of false gods was tolerated and encouraged and the glory of the one true God was obscured. In the end, he gave himself to the worship of the false gods of his foreign wives.

Solomon's religious apostasy prepared the way for his moral deterioration. His father David had said: "The God of Israel said, the Rock of Israel spake to me, He that ruleth over men must be just, ruling in the fear of God" (2 Samuel 23:3, к.j.v.). Solomon came to the place that he had absolute power over the lives of his subjects. It has been said that power corrupts and that absolute power corrupts absolutely. Power corrupts unless the man who has power continually remembers that he who rules over men must be just, walking in the fear of the Lord. The rule of Solomon which had started out as he sought an understanding heart became in time an intolerable tyranny. Many of Solomon's public works were constructive undertakings that benefited the nation. But Solomon in his old age moved to a magnificence of living and an uncontrolled extravagance which meant that his people were taxed beyond their capacity to endure. The people had been willing to give free labor for the work on the temple, but Solomon instituted a system of forced labor which meant that his people were practically slaves of the throne. A people will always fight against slavery to a foreign power, but some of the great oppressions come when people are enslaved by rulers who are of their own flesh and blood. The beginning of opposition to Solomon came in the ranks of those who were forced to work in the hated corvée.

During the close of the reign of Solomon the military position of Israel began to deteriorate. David had left an empire in which the nations around Israel were either subject to Israel or were bound to her by friendly alliances. In particular he had defeated the Syrians and had established himself in Damascus. Solomon began with an alliance with Egypt cemented by his marriage to the daughter of Pharoah. But the dynasty in Egypt changed, and in the latter part of the reign of Solomon Egypt was giving shelter to the enemies of Solomon. David and Joab had built an army that was one of the great fighting forces of their time. But Solomon's army was more for show than for battle. Joab had conquered Edom and put garrisons there, but Solomon lost control of Edom and with it control of the trade routes through Edom (1 Kings 11:14-22). Solomon also lost control of Damascus and prepared the way for the growth of Syria as the great enemy of Northern Israel (1 Kings 11:23-25).

More serious than the loss of Syria and Edom was the growth of disaffection in Ephraim and the northern tribes. This was supported by the prophet Ahijah from Shiloh as a judgment of God on Solomon for his religious apostasy. When the death of Solomon came, Jereboam the son of Nebat was waiting in Egypt to be called back to appear as the leader of the ten tribes in their demand that Rehoboam lighten the load that his father had laid on them. The deepest tragedy of the reign of Solomon was that by his oppression of his subjects in the latter part of his reign he created the tensions that made inevitable the coming of the day when Ephraim would depart from Judah. Centuries later Isaiah the prophet of Judah felt that the most tragic event in the history of his people up to the time of the invasion of Assyria was when the ten tribes separated permanently from Judah (Isaiah 7:17).

The tragedy of Solomon is the tragedy of a man who grasps at the show of power and loses its substance. He came to the throne of Israel at a time of great opportunity. He started well as he walked in humility before God and with a deep sense of responsibility for his people. But somewhere in his career as king something happened to Solomon. He ceased to follow after the Lord with his whole heart. He forgot that he that ruleth over men must be just, walking in the fear of the Lord. He tried to combine with the worship of the one true God the building of places of worship to false gods. In doing this Solomon proved himself unworthy to reign as the anointed of the Lord, the instrument of God's redemptive purpose in the life of Israel. The God who had come to Solomon at Gibeon to strengthen him for his task came to him again in an act of judgment in which the ten tribes were taken from the house of David and the empire of David and Solomon became the kingdoms of Israel and Judah.

# 23

## DAVID—the greatest and most beloved of Israel's kings

*Scripture Background: Isaiah 55; Psalm 89*

". . . I will make with you an everlasting covenant,
   my steadfast, sure love for David.
Behold, I made him a witness to the peoples,
   a leader and commander for the peoples" (Isaiah 55:3-4).

We have looked at David in his relation to the people who stood around him. We have seen him as he revealed his faith in God in the various life situations which he faced as he dealt with the men and women who gathered around him. It is our purpose now to make a rapid survey of his life as a whole. This will enable us to see him in perspective. We are particularly interested in David in his relation to the Lord in the various stages of his life.

We start with the boy as he watches his father's sheep. David was the youngest of the eight sons of Jesse. It is easy to visualize the growing boy as he cared for his sheep in the pasture land around Bethlehem. We can think of him as he plays on his harp and sings the songs of Israel. We can watch him as he practices with his sling until he can send the rock with unerring aim to the target. We can live with him as in defense of his sheep he fights and kills a lion and a bear. His daring in these combats with the wild beasts is not unrelated to his faith in the Lord. It is in his faith that the battle is the Lord's that he has the courage to face the lion and the bear. We can be sure that the young David was keenly aware of the oppression of his people by the

Philistines, and that he dreamed of the time when he would take his place in the armies of Israel. It was while he was keeping his father's sheep that the Lord looked into the heart of David and found the man he wanted for the leader of his people Israel. The call of the Lord to David was given to him in a simple service in the home of his father by the prophet Samuel. It was then that David became fully aware of the destiny to which he had been summoned. Not long after this David was sent by his father to carry provisions to his brothers in the army of Saul. It was in his knowledge that he was the anointed of the Lord for the deliverance of his people that David dared to go out to do battle with Goliath of Gath.

The victory over Goliath marked the end of David's life as a boy in Bethlehem. He became Saul's armor-bearer. There was a time when Saul loved David and David loved and admired the man who was king of Israel. During this time there was formed a strong friendship between David and Jonathan, the oldest son of Saul. The story of the friendship of these two has never been surpassed in literature. While he was in the court of Saul, David began to show his ability as a leader of men. When the representatives of all the tribes of Israel came to David to make him king, they said to him: "In times past, when Saul was king over us, it was you that led out and brought in Israel" (2 Samuel 5:2). It was because of the growing recognition of David as the real leader of Israel that the love of Saul for David turned to jealousy and hate. In this period of his life David married Michal, the daughter of Saul. This was a strange wedding, with Saul using his daughter in an effort to destroy David and David paying a dowry of two hundred dead Philistines. The life of David in the court of Saul ended abruptly with Saul's sending of soldiers to kill David in his home.

From the place of an officer of high rank in the court of Saul, David passed at once to the life of a fugitive. He fled first to Samuel at Ramah. Saul followed him, and David was saved by a strange experience in which Saul found himself among the prophets and prophesying before Samuel. From Samuel, David went to Jonathan in an effort to be sure that there was no possibility of a reconciliation with Saul and a return to his court. When Jonathan realized that his father was determined to kill David, we have the beautiful scene in which Jonathan and David renewed their covenant before the Lord, and David went forth as a lonely fugitive. He went first to Ahimelech, the high priest at Nob. He arrived alone, hungry and weaponless. He went forth with the loaves of the shewbread to sustain him on his journey and with the sword of Goliath in his hand. But his visit had tragic consequences for the priests at Nob.

David sought sanctuary among the Philistines in Gath, but the lonely fugitive was not welcome, and it was only by feigning madness that David was able to make his escape into the land of Judah. He went to the stronghold of Adullam. This was not far from Bethlehem, and it was here that David began to gather around him the men who were destined to become the greatest fighting unit in Israel's history. His own people came to him because they did not feel safe from the wrath of Saul. Among them were the sons of Zeruiah—Joab, Abishai, and Asahel. On the advice of the prophet Gad, David and his men left the cave of Adullam to hide in the wilderness in the south of Judah. It is from this period that we have the stories of David refusing to lift his hand against Saul as the Lord's anointed. The story of Nabal and of David's marriage to Abigail also belongs to this period.

The period in which David was a fugitive in the wilderness was followed by a brief time in which David and his men sought sanctuary among the Philistines and were settled at Ziklag. Achish, the king of the Philistines, would have liked to have David and his men as his bodyguard. It was common practice for kings to have foreign mercenaries serve in this way, for such men would not be involved in the intrigues of the court. In a similar manner Ittai the Gittite and a band of Philistines later served in David's court (2 Samuel 15:19-21). It was at the end of his stay in the land of the Philistines that David and his men rescued their wives and children from the Amalekites and wrought such destruction upon these desert robbers that they were never again a threat to Israel. In this early period of his life, David bears himself in such a manner that the approval of the Lord rests upon him.

The sojourn among the Philistines was followed by David's rule for seven years as king of Judah. During this time David was engaged in a long conflict with the house of Saul under the leadership of Abner. This was a war in which Abner was trying to establish the rule of Ishbosheth. It was a war which David could not afford to lose but did not want to win. He had no desire to establish his authority over all Israel at the point of the sword. He wanted to wait until the representatives of the tribes came to him of their own accord to offer him the throne. The deaths of Abner and Ishbosheth opened the way for David to become king of Judah and Israel.

The first years of David's reign over all Israel were among the most creative of his life. He seized Jerusalem from the Jebusites and made it his capital. He fought two decisive battles with the Philistines and so completely defeated them that never again were they to become a threat to Israel. When the nations on the east of Jordan became alarmed at the growth of Israel, David fought victorious wars with Ammon, Edom, and Moab, and more remarkably with the Syrians of Damascus and Zobah. He established the worship of the Lord at Jerusalem. We pause here to pay a tribute to the tremendous impact of David on Israel and through Israel on the whole world through his psalms written for the worship of the Lord. We do not have to enter into detailed debates concerning the authorship of individual psalms to recognize the creative contribution of David to the worship of Israel. The faith of David in the Lord as expressed in his psalms is still a rich resource of devotional literature.

We move at once to the period in David's life which was clouded by his sin with Bathsheba and by his attempt to cover his sin by bringing about the death of Uriah at the hands of the Ammonites. This was the dark side of the life of David. In this experience he was in no sense a man of whom God could approve. The deepest dimension of his sin was the way in which he had despised the word of the Lord. It is to David's credit, however, that he responded to the word of the Lord through

Nathan the prophet with a deep experience of repentance and confession of guilt. He bore the retribution which came as a consequence of his sin as a child of God. In this period of David's life we have his grief over the death of his infant son. The breakdown of the inner life of his home is shown by Amnon's rape of Tamar and Absalom's murder of Amnon. Then followed Absalom's banishment and David's yearning for his banished son. The word of the Lord spoken to David in his sin has become the instrument of the encounter of God with other men in their time of sin and failure. We see here both a word of judgment and a word of forgiveness when repentance is genuine.

The retribution which came to David for his sin reached its climax in Absalom's rebellion. The story of David as his son seeks his life is one of the great stories of Scripture. It is here that we see David in his readiness to accept without complaint the judgment of God. It is here that we have unforgettable pictures of the love and devotion to David of many of those around him. And it is here that we see the struggle in his soul between his wrath at the treachery of his son and his love for the young man Absalom. The story of David in this portion of his life touches the deepest emotions of which the human heart is capable.

We do not know much of the life of David after the rebellion of Absalom. It is in this period that we must put the story of his sin in taking the census. While we cannot be certain of what actually happened, the probability is that we have the rising in Israel of a spirit of conquest. It begins with some of the people and calls forth the wrath of the Lord. David himself becomes involved in the sin of using the power of the throne for the extortion of his people and in the sin of dreaming of using the great power of Israel for further ventures of military conquest. But regardless of the real nature of his sin, we can say that David repents when the word of the Lord comes to him and that he bears the punishment involved as one who never doubts the goodness and mercy of the Lord.

In his old age David impresses us as a man whose energy has

run out. He gives the appearance of a man who wants nothing more than to be let alone. But in a time of crisis such as that which arises when Adonijah attempts to seize the throne, he can arouse himself and act with wisdom and decision. He lives to see his son Solomon seated on the throne. He charges Solomon, saying: "I am about to go the way of all the earth. Be strong, and show yourself a man, and keep the charge of the LORD your God, walking in his ways and keeping his statutes, his commandments, his ordinances, and his testimonies . . ." (1 Kings 2:2-3).

When we look at the life of David as a whole we can say that he is probably the best known and the most beloved man in the Old Testament period. We have preserved in the Scriptures a wealth of biographical material concerning David. When we live with this material we can feel that we know this man of three thousand years ago better than we know many of the people with whom we are closely associated in our contemporary world. As we live with David we find that we are in contact with a man whose faith in the Lord points always to the reality of the God who raised him up and was with him in the whole of his earthly pilgrimage. The God of David is the God who confronts us in the context of our earthly life. When the great prophet of the Exile wishes to issue again God's call to his people he pictures the God of Israel as he says:

"Incline your ear, and come to me;
   hear, that your soul may live;
and I will make with you an everlasting covenant,
   my steadfast, sure love for David" (Isaiah 55:3).

The God who has revealed his love and mercy in the life of David is the God who invites us to come to him and promises to establish an everlasting covenant with us.

# 24

# THE CHRIST—Son of David and the Lord's Anointed

*Scripture Background: 2 Samuel 7; Luke 1:26—2:21*

"And the Lord God will give to him the throne of his father David" (Luke 1:32).

What does David have to do with the Christ? A thousand years of human history came between the age of David and the time of the coming of the Christ. What relation can there be between David and Jesus? When we ask this question we need to examine the references to David in the stories of the birth of Jesus. As Luke introduces us to Mary, he says that she is a virgin living in the village of Nazareth and betrothed to a man named Joseph, of the house of *David* (Luke 1:26-27). When the angel Gabriel makes his announcement to Mary he says of the son whom she will bear:

> "He will be great, and will be called the Son of
> the Most High;
> and the Lord God will give to him *the throne of his*
> *father David,*
> and he will reign over the house of Jacob for ever;
> and of his kingdom there will be no end" (Luke 1:32-33).

When John the Baptist is born, his father Zechariah is filled with the Holy Spirit and prophesies, saying:

> "Blessed be the Lord God of Israel,
> for he has visited and redeemed his people,
> and has raised up a horn of salvation for us

in *the house of his servant David,*
as he spoke by the mouth of his holy prophets from
   of old,
that we should be saved from our enemies,
and from the hand of all who hate us;
to perform the mercy promised to our fathers,
and to remember his holy covenant,
the oath which he swore to our father Abraham, to
   grant us
that we, being delivered from the hand of our enemies,
might serve him without fear,
in holiness and righteousness before him all the days
   of our life" (Luke 1:68-75).

When the angels announce to the shepherds the birth of Jesus they say: "To you is born this day *in the city of David* a Savior, who is Christ the Lord" (Luke 2:11). When the Wise Men ask where the Christ is to be born they are told that the prophet has foretold his birth in Bethlehem of Judea (Matthew 2:5). In the prophecy of Micah (Micah 5:2), the prediction of the birth of the Christ in Bethlehem is part of his identification with the poor and the humble. But the people of Israel would not forget that Bethlehem was also the birthplace of David.

When Jesus is grown to manhood and performs miracles of healing, the people are amazed and say: "Can this be *the Son of David?*" (Matthew 12:23). It is obvious that "Son of David" is one of the terms for the Messiah. When blind Bartimaeus calls to Jesus he says: *"Jesus, Son of David,* have mercy on me!" (Mark 10:47). And the question with which Jesus puts to silence the Pharisees calls forth from them the assertion that the Christ is to be the son of *David* (Matthew 22:41-46).

How did David become so deeply involved in the expectation of the Christ? When we read the books of Samuel, we should realize that both David and Saul are referred to as the Lord's anointed. The word "Messiah" means the anointed. And the word "Christ" is the Greek translation of the Hebrew word "Messiah." David thought of Saul as one whom the Lord had raised up for the deliverance of his people. He was not willing to take the life of Saul because he would not lift his hand against the Lord's anointed. And when David was anointed by Samuel his contemporaries began to think of him as the Lord's anointed, as a man raised up by God for the salvation of his people.

We find in the stories of David the conflict between the people's desire for a king who would be like the kings of the nations around about them and the concern of the Lord for a king who would be a man after his own heart and obedient to his will. The basic failure of Saul was his disobedience to the word of the Lord. It was because he had rejected the word of the Lord that he was rejected as king.

David fulfilled the concept of the king as the anointed of the Lord. He was the instrument of God for the deliverance of the children of Israel from their enemies, and he did establish the kingdom of Israel and lay the foundations for the golden age of Israel's history. When David came to the throne of Israel, the children of Israel were divided among themselves, in political bondage to the Philistines, and constantly threatened with invasion by the nations around about them. In a brief time David changed all this and lifted the kingdom of Israel to a place of power among the nations of the ancient world. In the days after they had been conquered by their enemies, the Jews never forgot the glory of the empire of David and Solomon.

But David did more than winning for the children of Israel victory over all their enemies. He set before his contemporaries and before all who should follow him the pattern of a king anointed of the Lord and obedient to the word of the Lord. We must not idealize the character of David. No one defends him in the matter of Uriah the Hittite. In this, the thing that David did displeased the Lord, but we can realize the depth and genuineness of David's repentance. David was a man of his time who in many ways fell below the pattern of what a man ought to be in the light of the teachings of Jesus. He was cruel in his treatment of his enemies who were outside the family of Israel. And he sinned in the matter of the numbering of the people. But in the broad sweep of his life David was a king who ruled over men in the fear of the Lord. It was because he walked in the ways of the Lord that the Lord promised to make for him a sure house and to establish his throne forever (2 Samuel 7:16).

David never turned aside to the worship of false gods. He established the worship of the Lord at Jerusalem. He lived in a world that was filled with the worship of false gods, but he never gave himself to the worship of the gods of the nations around about Israel and he never degraded the worship of the Lord by seeking to worship the one true God through images. The faith of David was that of a man who worshiped the Lord with his whole heart.

As men looked back upon David, he seemed to set for them the pattern of a king who reigned in the fear of the Lord. At the close of Browning's *Luria,* Tiburzio says:

> "A people is but the attempt of many
> To rise to the completer life of one;
> And those who live as models for the mass
> Are singly of more value than they all.
>
> . . . . . . .
>
> Keep but God's model safe, new men will rise
> To take its mould . . ."

Part of the significance of David for the whole life of Israel is to be found in the way in which he set the pattern of a great king who walked humbly in the way of the Lord. Other kings of the house of Judah were judged against the pattern found in David. When Solomon in his old age gave himself to the worship of the gods of his foreign wives, it was written of him that "his heart was not wholly true to the LORD his God, as was the heart of David his father" (1 Kings 11:4). Of Asa, the grandson of Rehoboam, it was said that he "did what was right in the eyes of the LORD, as David his father had done" (1 Kings 15:11). Of Josiah it was written that "he did what was right in the eyes of the LORD, and walked in all the way of David his father" (2 Kings 22:2). In the whole history of Judah her kings were judged by whether they did, or did not, walk in the ways of David, the founder of the dynasty.

When the word of the Lord came to Jeroboam the son of Nebat concerning his selection as the man to be king over Northern Israel, he was promised that the Lord would build him a sure house if he would walk in the pattern of obedience to the Lord that had already been set by David (1 Kings 11:38). But instead, Jeroboam corrupted the worship of the Lord by teaching the people to worship the God of Israel through the golden calves which he set up in Bethel and in Dan. And in contrast to David, Jeroboam is branded as the man who "made Israel to sin."

The significance of David runs deeper than that of being the man who set the pattern of the righteous king. David in his own generation was known as the Lord's anointed. He was thought of as a man raised up by God and empowered of God to deliver his people from their enemies and to lead them into their destiny as the people of God. And as the children of Israel became again and again subject to foreign powers they began to hope and to pray that God would send them another leader who in the pattern set by David would break the power of their enemies and enable them to enter into their destiny. This hope is beautifully expressed by Zechariah in the passage from Luke we have already quoted. He describes the Christ as a horn of salvation raised up of God in the house of his servant David. The messianic hope in Israel took its pattern in part from the memory of David as the Lord's anointed who in his generation delivered his people from their enemies and established a kingdom in which they might worship the Lord in holiness and righteousness.

In time the word "Messiah," which in David's time could be used of anyone who was anointed with oil for the service of the Lord, came to be used almost exclusively of the One whom the Lord would send to be the deliverer of his people. The hope of the coming of the Messiah was nourished by the predictions of the prophets. And at the time of Jesus' birth the messianic expectancy was at white heat. When John came preaching we are told that "the people were in expectation, and all men questioned in their hearts concerning John, whether perhaps he were the Christ" (Luke 3:15). And the delegation from Jerusalem which came to John wanted to know whether or not he was the Christ (John 1:19-20).

In the time of David, there was a conflict between the popular demand for a king like the kings of the nations around about Israel and the divine concern for a king who would be obedient to the word of the Lord. By the time of Jesus, the Jews had corrupted the hope of the coming of the Lord's anointed. The people had passed over the emphasis on a person who would be obedient to the word of the Lord and had concentrated on the hope for a person raised up by God to deliver them from their enemies and to establish them in a dominant position in their world.

Jesus definitely claimed to be the Christ (John 4:26; Matthew 16:13-23; Mark 14:61-62). He came as One sent by God to be the Savior of his people. But he did not come to be the kind of Messiah his people were expecting. He blended with the concept of the Messiah the picture of the suffering servant given in Isaiah. He was the Christ, but he was the Christ who must suffer and die. Jesus did not come as a military conqueror. He claimed the allegiance of men not because he had defeated them in battle but because they had responded in faith, love, and obedience to his disclosure of himself. He did not come to be a political deliverer. He came to save his people from their sins. He did not come to re-establish the throne of David at Jerusalem. He came to establish a kingdom that was in this world but not of this world. He came to call men to an eternal salvation. He came to bind to himself a people of God who would be with him forever. In the coming of the Christ, the promise that the Lord would establish the throne of David forever (2 Samuel 7:16) received a fulfillment that goes beyond anything that ever entered into the mind of David or of his contemporaries.

The kingdom which the crucified and risen Lord has established is a mighty power in our world today. There are millions who acknowledge Jesus as Lord and seek to serve him. He rules over the people of God, and those who serve him are confident that "of his kingdom there will be no end" (Luke 1:33). They believe that the God who raised up David has given to great David's Greater Son "the name which is above every name, that at the name of Jesus every knee should bow . . . and every tongue confess that Jesus Christ is Lord, to the glory of God the Father" (Philippians 2:9-11).